Roadmap for Success

Guideline for Small Business Operations

Winston Thompson, MBA, CPA

Copyright © 2024

All Rights Reserved

Dedication

I would like to dedicate this book to my children [Mark, Kadeem, and Imani] and to all family members and Business Associates who have provided me with a source of strength and care. To all of you, this book represents a ROADMAP, not just for business but concepts for planning your daily lives. If you don't have a plan to Succeed, then you have an automatic plan to fail.

Get a ROADMAP FOR SUCCESS!

Acknowledgment

I would like to take a moment to express my deepest gratitude and appreciation to the incredible partners and associates who supported the Thompson & Company Group for many years, especially Ebenezer Anang, Joseph Aloi, Donnyell Bourgeois, and Brenda Pean. A Special thanks to members of our affiliated group of TAXPROS EXPRESS ADVISORS, namely Larry Mitchell, Alberto Alexander, Vikram Sharma, and Paresh Shah. Joseph Reid, Joseph Stephens, Magalie Derose. Doug Brown, Carole Colas, Atila Kiss Kindel James, and Rodney Littles. Additionally, special thanks to Michael Roberts, a Media Marketing professional who started with me and assisted with our first EBOOK, "ROADMAP FOR SUCCESS."

To all our Dedicated Clients around the country, thanks for your support. Expand and grow your business with the ROADMAP FOR SUCCESS.

About the Author

Winston Thompson is a Certified Public Accountant (CPA) who is an entrepreneur at heart. He is a business consultant and an auditor by profession. Winston helps entrepreneurs establish businesses and devise robust financial strategies. Also, he aids existent enterprises in their endeavor to grow and outpace competition through efficient and detailed business plans.

Preface

This book aims to allow small businesses to thrive through rigorous planning. Thompson's objective is to provide entrepreneurs with an opportunity to plan in a way that is future-proof and professional. Through his experience in auditing and business consulting, he aims to guide entrepreneurs—current and future ones—through important things when starting a new business.

An important aspect of the book is to emphasize why planning from scratch and in detail plays a crucial role in whether a business will survive in the future or not. The book shows how planning for various aspects beforehand and having contingencies in place will help save businesses from any untoward pressures, bring down tax bills, and reduce tax reductions. Thompson's years of experience guiding businesses means he is well-equipped to write this guide with authority.

If you have a business or are planning to start one but have not given it enough thought, then you should pause for a moment and read this book. You need to know what important planning elements can help make or break your business. So, what are you waiting for? Begin evaluating your strategies and business through this book and save yourself from a disaster waiting to happen.

Contents

Dedication i
Acknowledgment ii
About the Author iii
Preface iv
Chapter 1: Start the Journey Toward Success 1
Chapter 2: Our Roadmap for Success 16
Step 1: The Business Model 30
Chapter 3: Introduction 31
Chapter 4: Direct Sales 47
Chapter 5: Franchise Model 58
Chapter 6: Freemium Model 73
Chapter 7: Subscription Model 85
Step 2: A Financing Strategy 100
Chapter 8: Importance of a Financing Strategy .. 101
Chapter 9: Cash Flow Management 120
Chapter 10: Planning for Purchases 137
Chapter 11: Big Picture Considerations 153
Chapter 12: Raising Capital 165
Step 3: Marketing System 176
Chapter 13: Introduction 177
Chapter 14: Affiliate Marketing Plan 194
Chapter 15: Social Media Marketing Plan 206
Chapter 16: Community-based Marketing Plan 219
Step 4: Cost Cutting System 228
Chapter 17: Importance of Cost Cutting 229
Chapter 18: Cost Saving 247
Chapter 19: CFO Services 269
Step 5: Tax Reduction Plan 284
Chapter 20: Introduction 285
Chapter 21: Tax Planning Strategies 300
Step 6: Wealth Accumulation and Protection System 306
Chapter 22: Introduction 307
Chapter 23: Rising Economic Inequity for Small Business 319
Chapter 24: CARES Act 331
Step 7: A Health and Wellness System 342

Chapter 25: Introduction 343
Chapter 26: Wellness Strategies 361

Chapter 1: Start the Journey Toward Success

The Apple logo is recognizable whether you're on a busy New York City street or a rural rust belt highway. You can easily distinguish Apple products from others in an instant. Hence, it is safe to say Apple has accomplished more than just becoming the leader in technology. The business has achieved what many startups nowadays can only dream of — a shining legacy that might outlast everyone alive today and remain in the consciousness of future generations for a very long time.

Apple did not stumble upon success overnight, however. It had a solid vision from the get-go and made it extremely clear to people what it wanted to achieve in the technological sphere. In order to gain some insight into its huge success, it is imperative that we shine a light on its beginnings.

In 1976, Apple was founded by Steve Jobs, Steve Wozniak, and Ronald Wayne to sell Wozniak's first hand-built personal computer named Apple 1.

The Apple 1 was sold as a motherboard with a CPU, RAM, and basic textual-video chips. It lacked a built-in keyboard, monitor, case, and other Human Interface Devices.

The Apple 1 was released in July 1976 and retailed for around $700. Shortly after the release of the device, Wayne left the company and exited while pocketing around $800.

In 1977, Apple launched the Apple 2 and disrupted the personal computer industry. It had a much easier-to-use interface and colored graphics. The company grew from under a million dollars in revenue to a hundred million by 1980.[1]

The '80s were the decade of stiff competition from IBM and Microsoft in the corporate computing market. The Apple 3 came and went without much fanfare since it had a lot of technical glitches.

When Steve Jobs left Apple in 1985, it had almost a hundred million dollars in yearly revenue, and when he returned for his second stint in 1996, he faced a company that was on the brink of collapse.

His focus upon returning was restructuring the entire company, dropping costly and unnecessary projects, and aligning the company's goals. He emphasized changing how products were developed and transforming the organizational structure.

Business history and organizational theory argue that as entrepreneurial firms expand and become more complicated, they must switch from a

---

[1] https://www.feedough.com/the-history-of-apple/

functional to a multidivisional structure to align accountability and control and avoid the chaos that results when many decisions are made at the top of the organizational chart.

The view holds that giving business unit leaders complete authority over crucial tasks helps them take the best possible action to satisfy the customers' demands within their specific units, maximize their outcomes, and allow the executives overseeing them ease in evaluating their performance.

Apple demonstrated that a traditional multidivisional strategy was incompatible with their field of work and industry and that businesses facing massive disruptions in their line of work may profit from a functional structure.

Apple's dedication to a functional organization does not imply that its organizational structure has remained stagnant since its implementation. That structure has changed as the significance of artificial intelligence, deep learning, and other emerging fields has grown.

Here, we shall explain how Apple's particular organizational structure fosters creativity and effectiveness, which may be helpful for people and businesses looking to flourish in quickly transforming and disruptive environments.

Why a Functional Approach?

The primary goal of Apple is to provide goods that improve people's daily lives. That entails consistently inventing both within existing product categories as well as creating wholly new ones, like the iPhone and the Apple Watch. The iPhone camera, probably more than any other product feature, best exemplifies Apple's dedication to ongoing innovation.

Apple uses a framework centered on functional knowledge to produce such advancements. Its basic tenet is that decision-making authority should always rest with those who have the most knowledge and experience in a certain field. It is much easier and simpler to balance costs incurred in developing a particular product and the value provided to the end-user when people with deep expertise are making the decisions. It is completely different from organizations where general managers are primarily held accountable for meeting numerical targets. A functional approach provides authority and autonomy to an expert; decisions taken are based on that approach.

Ever since Steve Jobs introduced the functional approach to Apple, every manager has been expected to possess two leadership qualities:

1. Wide-ranging Expertise

Early on, Steve Jobs embraced the idea of management being experts in their field. In a 1984 interview, Jobs stated that Apple had hired a professional management team to run operations, but that experiment failed. Since then, the approach of experts leading experts was introduced, where specialists could create a pool of people with deep know-how and learn from one another.

These specialists would be dispersed amongst several product lines if Apple were structured into business units. As a result, their ability to jointly solve issues and develop and improve ideas would be diminished.

2. Immersion in Details

Many organizations insist that attention to detail is a priority in their daily business operations, but only a few organizations can match Apple. Apple products are all a result of extreme details, reflected in every nook and cranny of the devices.

Even a matter of reducing highlights on the curvature of their phones isn't simply a matter of a mathematical formula but a constant emphasis on improvement and betterment, which is spilled over to the lower tiers of management and workers as well.

Having leaders who are authorities in their respective fields and can dig deep into the specifics has a profound effect on the turnaround of products and the company's running. Leaders can press, enquire, and "smell" a problem far before it even emerges, are aware of the crucial details, and can make smarter decisions while allocating resources. Working with experts who offer better direction and mentoring than a general manager is liberating and has been appreciated by employees at the company.

Post-Jobs Era

Since his passing in 2011, the post-Jobs era hasn't been without its successes. Some people feel that Apple has become solely iterative in its tech releases rather than the transformative company it was in the beginning. The company has, however, been a huge success since Tim Cook took over as CEO.

Apple still has the most integrated ecosystem in the market and has reached a market capitalization of $2 trillion in 2022.

The challenges faced by many businesses today are the kinds relating to roadmaps or approaches to developing in order to survive in a competitive environment. Small businesses in this regard face the possibility of going extinct without implementing a sustainable and modern operations management system.

Now, from the perspective of a small business, let's take a look at the imminent need and challenges of modernizing strategy and operations.

The Small Business Perspective

A small business requires a lot of work to get started. Even after your business has taken off, it may be challenging to stay current with technological advancements and maintain its competitive edge. This is particularly true when your competitors have larger budgets to work with, giving them the financial resources to investigate new possibilities and make the most of emerging platforms.

However, there is another way to look at it: smaller, more agile businesses can stay on their toes, whereas larger businesses are frequently at a disadvantage because they are constrained by expensive legacy technologies that are too expensive to modernize.

There are ways and means of modernizing and ensuring your business operates well without breaking the bank. To maintain successful growth, small business owners must utilize the possibilities provided by contemporary software, tools, and services. Here are some doable suggestions to help keep your company abreast of the current technology and keep you one step ahead of your rivals.

Bridging the Physical and the Digital

The main concern for small businesses is the fear of transitioning from a mom-and-pop store to selling inventory online or through an e-commerce website. The thought of selling online, the initial investment, and the regular upkeep are so daunting that most businesses stay away from this altogether.

Customers nowadays are doing more and more of their shopping online, and the pandemic had a big impact on online sales and the emphasis on contactless deliveries and payments.

An online storefront with the physical store in combination will help provide an option to a potential customer and will also save time and hassle of coming to the store if distance or health is a factor in the purchase.

Switching to Cloud-based Solutions

Small businesses frequently keep droves of paper records such as invoices, contracts, and receipts in inefficient and cumbersome filing cabinets. A particular file can take a lot of time and resources to be found. Small businesses might feel it is better to have a physical copy rather than trust something they can't see or watch. What needs to be launched is a massive trust-building campaign between business owners and the solution providers. Small business owners should be apprised of the advantages of having important and historical documents on a cloud server rather than dealing with the costs associated with keeping documents from decaying and making photocopies for future use.

Since many of these services are based on small monthly or yearly membership fees rather than significant up-front expenditures, transferring data to cloud-based technology is technologically and financially feasible for most businesses. Using a mobile device to edit and distribute cloud-based documents eliminates the need to move paper documents around the office physically.

Of course, cloud services are more than just virtual file vaults. The inherent analytics and machine learning capabilities of this internet technology are also advantageous since they give business owners access to useful information and helpful intelligence across a variety of activities.

Automation

You might be worried about the impending AI apocalypse, in which our shrewd robot overlords will violently overthrow us. However, the ineffectiveness of attempting to finish all your everyday duties in anything resembling a fair amount of time should be enough to persuade small business operators to innovate.

We like to pretend that we are experts on the customer journey as business owners. After all, doing things right is what we do best. Unfortunately, many only give lip service to the customer experience and forego real route mapping because they think they can put themselves "in the client's shoes."

Customer journey mapping focuses on depicting the consumer's experience from the first point of contact to the point of sale and, ideally, on to the creation of a devoted long-term relationship. With this crucial knowledge at their disposal, business owners can provide better customer service based on data analytics provided by an artificially intelligent system.

Marketing

Many businesses lack the advertising and media budgets to market their products effectively, which can produce instant results. Small businesses usually rely on the business of proximity. The return or main customers live near the area or in the same town, and the business is an unknown entity outside that city or district. There are several methods of promoting your business without causing too much damage to the company's bottom line:

- Pay per Click Advertising
- Inviting influencers to promote your business online.

- Promoting your business on social media on your official business page
- Exploring Cross-promotion with businesses operating in different sectors

In the next section, we shall explore a suggested roadmap that small businesses can follow in order to maximize their growth and improve their profitability in times of uncertainty and disruption.

Small Business Success Roadmap

The tasks are never-ending for small business owners. Because of this, setting priorities and doing the correct things with your time is just as critical as maintaining a full calendar each day, if not more so. Because of this, success in business depends on laying the groundwork for a roadmap for success. One of the fantastic benefits of owning your own business is being your own boss. You can set your hours, work from anywhere, pursue topics you're interested in, and much more.

Despite how wonderful it is, working for yourself or operating your own business also causes unneeded worry and anxiety. Fortunately, there are methods that can make it easier for you to keep up with everything. Not only to do it properly and have room for that new pastime but also to stay sane.

Controlling Your Schedule

Everyone has the same 24 hours. But your calendar is typically extremely busy if you own a small business. To overcome your anxiety in this situation, keep in mind that only you can manage your schedule and work things around for yourself. Superior time management abilities are the key to it all, so time blocking, prioritization, and reducing distractions are the way to go.

Standing Out in a Crowded Market

Differentiating yourself from the competition is the key to standing out. Create a Unique Selling Proposition (USP) for your brand if you want to stand out from the competition. But not just any—your USP needs to connect with both you and your audience.

Start by defining your specialty and target market as part of your business success roadmap. Focus on how your product or service alters a person's ability to live their life. The product should ideally resolve an issue that a customer is facing, and that can be considered a valuable addition. Follow this by thoroughly researching your rivals. Here, you can compare your product or service against others' by putting them side by side. During this practice, if your points of differentiation aren't obvious, you're either not being unique enough, or you haven't done enough research.

Patience and Focus

Maintaining focus on a predetermined objective is essential when beginning a new business venture in order to gauge success. You must decide on the overarching objective and then designate more manageable checkpoints along the road. Making a "to-do list" every night before bed and working on it first thing in the morning is highly advised to help you stick to a schedule and stay focused. But in order to avoid setting yourself up for failure, it is crucial to create a realistic to-do list.

Besides the aforementioned points, it is also crucial to possess resilience in order to handle both daily difficulties and the patience required to meet expectations for overall business performance. Noting that it can take years for a firm to reach its full potential and become a small business success story, it is important to remember that the majority of successful enterprises are not created overnight.

Onboarding Resources That Fit

Making difficult decisions could apply to this category as well, but it is imperative for an organization to have team players. All successful small businesses share one thing in common: they are aware that their ability to hire the right people will be crucial to their success. More than in big businesses, every employee in a small business needs to be trusted to handle his or her daily obligations with the least amount of supervision.

To reduce overhead costs, the hiring structure must be as efficient as possible. As a result, no small business can afford to waste a position by recruiting the wrong person. However, the converse scenario also applies. A stellar employee's departure is unaffordable for any small organization. Developing your staff and giving them respect encourages growth and reduces employee turnover in the long run.

It is clear how important a roadmap is for business success, especially for small businesses. If you have a properly crafted roadmap in place, your business can easily tackle any obstacle that comes its way. This is where Thompson & Company's *Roadmap for Success* comes into play. Thompson & Company is a New York-based professional accounting firm that offers its services to a range of entities, including expert financial and investment services, small businesses, non-profits, and individuals. Founded over 32 years ago, the company has cemented itself as one of the leading accounting firms in New York, with a proven track record of providing its clients with outstanding financial services.

With the primary goal of providing competent and insightful advice to clients to allow them to make informed business decisions, Thompson & Company has introduced the *Roadmap for Success,* a revolutionary integrated system that serves as a guide for small businesses seeking success.

Encompassing a combination of disciplines, techniques, and tools, *Roadmap for Success* is a comprehensive system designed to help small businesses plan, organize, market, operate, and streamline their operations to maximize profits.

Conclusion

Adapting to newer technologies and processes will help you save money, streamline your operations, and increase your Return on Investment (ROI) if you want to stay ahead of the curve or even satisfy the demands of a contemporary market. Businesses that are prepared technologically and ready to adapt when a valuable new software or system is developed and introduced will always be in the best position to expand. Since "it's not the big that eats the small, it's the fast that eats the slow."

While business success is not something impossible to attain, the reason many companies fall behind is that they don't have the vision or the right direction to move forward and need a little guidance. In today's modern world, where anything you need help with can easily be found with a tap of your finger, don't hesitate to reach out for it if you feel like you need guidance to attain business success. After all, a little help never hurt anybody!

Chapter 2: Our Roadmap for Success

If you are thinking about starting your own business or have previously done so, you must be aware of the emotional roller coaster and the strong pull of freedom and exhilaration that comes with the decision to do so. Despite all the difficulties young businesses encounter, lacking passion is not one of them. Entrepreneurs are fervent believers who are renowned for being motivated and upbeat. These characteristics are essential because starting a successful business can be extremely challenging. Successful entrepreneurs rely on strong convictions and faith to get them through hard days and unforeseen difficulties.

Entrepreneurial passion is more than an internal emotional state. It is a booming industry, as evidenced by the many books, magazines, websites, products, and services that cater to people's passion for running their own businesses. It eradicates the gap between passion and entrepreneurship and helps would-be founders to follow their dreams. With enough desire and commitment, anything seems possible. Disenchantment with large employers, not getting promotions, and relative unhappiness in a line of work indicate that running a small business may be the best way to move forward.

When Pamela Slim, the best-selling author of *Escape from Cubicle Nation: From Corporate Prisoner to Thriving Entrepreneur*, established her blog in 2004 of the same name, it struck a chord with the tens of millions of individuals who were desperate to quit their corporate positions and pursue their interests. These disillusioned individuals had persevered and worked in industries that sometimes didn't pay well, made them work long hours, and were not able to provide job satisfaction. In the past, people would stick to their employers because they would provide relative stability in a sometimes-unexpected economic environment. But, over the past two decades, due to economic changes that have led to wave after wave of unemployment, even this safety net has vanished.

Corporate America's once-lauded safety net for people has now become as obsolete as the rotary phone. Unfortunately, there is a big gap between what entrepreneurs accomplish and their level of desire. The majority of newly launched enterprises collapse within a few years. Even venture-backed firms that are run by brilliant founders with above-average ideas can fail. Apart from that, business owners who *do* make it through the first few years aren't always in a happy place. The typical new business owner puts in more hours, experiences more stress, and makes much less money over ten years than if they had stayed in their former position.

Starting a new business requires exceptional levels of commitment and hard work. An entrepreneur does not go home at 5 p.m. The work is never-ending, the future looks uncertain, and the number of responsibilities is endless. A business does not become a success story overnight. There is no magical moment where you wake up to a booming business without putting in the necessary effort. In order to create a successful business, you need commitment, dedication, and willingness to do whatever it takes to achieve success.

It is also important that an individual establishes a mental sketch or roadmap before embarking on an entrepreneurial journey. Here are some tips for self-evaluation that can help start a new business with a bang:

- **Start a Dialogue with Yourself:** Start by posing some fundamental inquiries to yourself: Who am I? What do I excel at? What do the people who matter to me think of me? When did I last feel truly alive? What can I learn from people who are inspirational to me and who have a clear purpose? Such self-awareness cultivates drive, self-assurance, and self-esteem that can make a person an unstoppable force and embeds perseverance that helps them keep going even in the face of failure and hardship.

- **Identifying Inner Strengths:** Before starting an entrepreneurial venture, you need to be aware of your strengths and weaknesses. Often, we possess many more strengths than we realize, and it takes a little digging to understand what we are truly capable of.

The questions to ask yourself should be: *What skills have I always possessed? What things am I good at? What inspires and drives me?* Certain skills might come naturally to you, and, at the same time, other things might take some time to develop.

Studies have also shown that people should take more risks in their choices and decisions. People rarely go out of their comfort zone to pursue something they think they lack the required skills in. This can be counter-productive when a situation arises that requires you to step out of your safe zone and handle several different aspects of business that you may never have encountered before. Facing unexpected challenges is what being an entrepreneur is all about, and in the long term, people can find themselves enjoying and succeeding in different business roles in which they initially had no confidence or the desire to pursue.

- **Know Where You Add Value**: Working in a job you are skilled at but don't enjoy is not a means to find contentment. You can better focus on the chances, responsibilities, and career routes where success is likely to emerge when you are aware of the skills that you already have and improve upon them. We all underestimate the capabilities, abilities, and knowledge accumulated gradually over time. Finding problems you can help resolve in your business is a terrific way to learn where you can add value and, in the process, identify the issues you are enthusiastic about and the difficulties you like tackling.

The answer to these questions can help you bolster your strengths and, as a result, make you a well-rounded individual.

The Amazon Success Story

Amazon. This multi-billion-dollar entity doesn't need an introduction. We have all heard of the Amazon marketplace, a global e-commerce network that connects suppliers and customers. You might be surprised to learn that the company has a wide range of goods in its portfolio, including Amazon Game Studios, Amazon Drive, a cloud storage service, and Amazon Web Services (AWS), a complete cloud platform utilized by many computer companies around the world.

The most lucrative shopping website on the internet, at the moment, is Amazon.com, which is more successful than Walmart and even eBay. How did Amazon achieve such great success? How did a budding businessman who initially focused on the book industry create a multi-billion-dollar empire?

Let's examine some elements that have shaped the success of Amazon:

1. Focus on Innovation

When it comes to implementing cutting-edge techniques and technologies, Amazon has been a leader. Examples include deploying robots to increase the effectiveness of e-commerce fulfillment operations or implementing AI applications in logistics, warehousing, and distribution.

Online buying with Alexa is also important to highlight. With Alexa, a voice assistant that enables customers to navigate their e-commerce trip with voice instructions rather than clicking a mouse or tapping a screen, Amazon explored brand-new opportunities for its customers.

Additionally, Jeff Bezos, the owner of Amazon, infused an innovative culture into Amazon's working environment. Employees can, therefore, test remarkable ideas without being afraid of failing. According to Bezos, failure is necessary to try new things. A constant reimagining of how things operate is key; with experience, things get better in the long term.

2. Unprecedented Customer Service

Amazon has long placed a high priority on providing exceptional customer service. Bezos wants to concentrate on the company's clients rather than its rivals, and this philosophy appears to be effective.

A properly laid out customer support page from Amazon enables a simple and quick search for the necessary information:

- Customers can view the status of active orders on the Order page and cancel them. They can use the information on this page to offer comments for the seller or the goods or to quickly resolve any difficulties.

- Customers can find answers to frequently asked questions about processing return and refund requests on the Return and Refund website.

- Six sections for managing user profiles are available on the Account page: Your Addresses, Login & Security, Your Payments, Gift Cards, Prime, and Your Orders.

3. Word-of-mouth Marketing

Despite the advancement of digital technology, Bezos thinks that word-of-mouth marketing is still vital in generating sales. The internet ecosystem increases the power of word-of-mouth. Businesses can reach or lose many more customers if they can physically discuss their satisfaction or discontent with a product or service with six or so other potential customers. It is, therefore, important for the company's frontline sales and customer support teams to provide current and potential clients with the best possible service available. Achieving this will help not only grow a loyal customer base but will also keep the existing customers intact and, therefore, lower the total customer acquisition cost.

Remember: Trial and Error Strategies Do Not Always Work

Consultants and academics have claimed for decades that the concept of sustainable competitive advantage, which is at the heart of strategy, has reached its end since the world has become extremely fast-paced, hypercompetitive, complicated, ambiguous, and uncertain. Competitive advantage is now fleeting and susceptible to disruption by players inside and outside of an industry.

Strategic agility or adaptability entails quick pivots, self-disruption, and a lot of experimentation and is a typical prescription for competing in the lack of a competitive edge. According to this mindset, success frequently involves strategic maneuvering as soon as new opportunities present themselves. The pitfall of this strategy is that it fails to address value-addition in the long term and is only focused on the present and now. Copying a competitor's business decision can harm your company in the short and long-term since every business structure is different and has unique caveats.

Today's companies need new sources of value-creation rather than rapid strategy change. Three components can lead to far more productive outcomes in the long term rather than mimicking what competitors might be doing:

- Foresight on how the sector will change in the future.
- Insight into the qualities that make the firm's assets and competencies unique and valuable.
- Cross-sight into how assets are now owned and externally available can be combined to produce value.

These components closely resemble the ways science has advanced. The more thoroughly thought out an idea is, the more likely it is to be validated by the tests that scientists design to assess its credibility. Less thought-out theories lead to more failures in the long term. This may be okay if your only objective is to develop and test new theories, but there is little question that conducting experiments on theories that are not fully developed is more inefficient than conducting experiments on theories that are. Furthermore, in business, where strategic experiments include significant financial outlays, experimentation without a strong grounding in strategy is a hugely value-destroying proposition.

Most leaders see themselves as doers rather than thinkers, but additional thinking is needed rather than additional doing.

The difference between strategic successes and failures has far more to do with the quality of the theory behind the company's strategic experiments than with the pace of the experimentation and trial and error. Sustaining value creation, by extension, requires better corporate theories — not faster-paced pivots. So, never make a business plan as you go along; that is just plain reckless.

Crucial Functions for Small Businesses

Many small enterprises fail, particularly during economic downturns. However, it has been observed that many fail due to their failure to hire key personnel across different functions.

Keeping multiple departments in charge of different organizational tasks is crucial even for a startup to divide responsibilities and function efficiently. Even though a small business might not require every department a big company has, a few are required to build a strong foundation.

Here are some of the departments that are crucial for small businesses:

Production

One of the most important departments for a small business includes the production department, which provides your service or product to your clients. Employees in this sector must be well-trained and adhere to strict protocols to produce high-quality items. If they perform their work subpar, you risk losing clients or tarnishing your reputation.

Sales

The sales department collaborates with marketing to help you sell more products and services. Leads are generated if your marketing department is doing its job. The leads can then be qualified and vetted by sales professionals. The sales department will make a more personal connection with customers and help them decide whether or not to purchase a product or service.

Sales professionals require customer service skills, but they may not be customer service representatives. Depending on your company, your salespeople may be responsible for providing customer service to their clients, but you may also choose a customer service department.

Marketing

A marketing department is required if you want to attract customers. Of course, you can outsource your marketing needs, but having a few people in-house to manage quick-turnaround projects, such as launching a new product or managing social media, may be necessary.

A marketing department can assist you in branding your company to stand out from the crowd in terms of competition. Marketing professionals also use large amounts of data to learn about their customers and devise strategies to help them find them online or in-store.

Thompson & Company Can Help Your Business

Thompson & Company's *Roadmap for Success* is a groundbreaking, integrated system that provides small businesses with a "how to" blueprint and roadmap that can lead to success.

After 32 years of helping small businesses grow and develop, we have completely re-invented the art of growing and sustaining small businesses. It is a system that combines assets from various disciplines, techniques, and tools into a comprehensive system designed to assist small businesses in planning, organizing, marketing, operating, and streamlining their operations in order to maximize profits. In fact, by implementing processes using our system, you can potentially **double your revenue in 12 to 18 months**.

However, it is important to remember that while effective, this is not a magic wand. You can only succeed with dedication, commitment, and willingness to follow our success plan.

The small business Roadmap for Success from Thompson & Company will take all the guesswork out of the process and provide you with the tools and guidance you need to succeed. It is not a one size fits all; at Thompson & Company, we devise a roadmap for you that fits your business's needs.

Conclusion

Starting a new business is exciting and stressful; you should prepare for the many milestones, stresses, failures, mistakes, and successes that will come your way. What you do in the days before you start your business can make all the difference.

Do not forget to accept feedback and constructive criticism, and be open to new ideas and the rapidly changing industry. Make use of modern technology, apps, social media, and the digital world. Staying up to date with market trends, digital marketing, and new ways to reach out to customers and run businesses will help you reach your goals.

It is a hard road that can be the most rewarding, and remember that a mistake is not a failure; the true failure is in giving up entirely, which is never an option because success is right around the corner.

The best business minds are a force to be reckoned with and do not get fazed by the economy's peaks and troughs. Their operational duties are fueled by integrity and immense passion for what they do. This is what separates them from the rest and what should separate you from your peers.

Step 1: The Business Model

Chapter 3: Introduction

As previously discussed, no business or individual can hope to attain success without a roadmap in place. Thompson & Company's roadmap for success consists of seven crucial steps, namely:

1. The Business Model
2. Financing Strategy
3. Marketing System
4. Cost Cutting System
5. Tax Reduction System
6. Wealth Accumulation and Protection System
7. Health and Wellness System

This chapter will focus on the first and most essential step: The Business Model.

The Business Model

The road to success in a highly competitive environment is arduous and full of challenges. This is why, even before taking the first steps, a company's business model should be well-established and robust enough to be able to face any headwinds that it might have to face in the short and the long term.

The term "Business Model" is thrown around a lot when discussing small businesses and startups. It is rather tricky to know which one best suits your business.

A business model's aim is to provide a solution to a problem that your target market/consumer is in at that moment, being better than the direct competitors and maintaining a balance between the company's costs and revenues.

The term "business model" refers to an organization's profit-making strategy. It specifies the products or services that the company intends to sell, its target market, and any anticipated expenses. Business models are critical for both new and established companies. They assist new and developing businesses in attracting investment, recruiting talent, and motivating management and staff.

Established businesses must update their business models on a regular basis, or they will fail to anticipate future trends and challenges. Business models also assist investors in evaluating companies of interest to them and employees in understanding the future of a company they may want to work for.

A business model is a sophisticated plan for running a profitable business in a specific market. The "value proposition" is a critical component of the business model. It describes a company's goods or services and why they are desirable to customers or clients, ideally stated in a way that distinguishes the product or service from its competitors.

When preparing the business model for a new venture, the first thing that needs to be addressed is the finalization of the corporate structure under which the organization is going to function. There are different corporate structures the venture could opt for based on its preferences. The various structures are **Sole Proprietorship, Partnership, Limited Liability Company (LLC), Corporation, Nonprofit Corporation**, and **Cooperative**.

The different structures could further be elaborated as follows:

- **Sole Proprietorship:** the most basic and noncomplex form of a business in which the entire business is owned and operated by one individual. All profits are solely entitled to the owner, who is also liable for all business debts and obligations.
- **Partnership:** This type of arrangement involves two or more people who share the ownership of the business. The profits, debts, and obligations are shared among the partners, and the proportion by which these are shared varies according to the nature of the partnership, i.e., in general partnerships, all the partners manage the business and share responsibility for the debts and losses. On the other hand, there is a limited partnership, in which there are both general partners and limited partners, with the limited ones sharing limited liability of the business.

- **Corporation:** it is a legal entity separate from the shareholders of the business. The perks included for an organization opting for this type of structure are that it offers the shareholders limited liability protection and that their personal assets are not at risk with the debts and obligations of the business.
- **Limited Liability Company (LLC):** It combines the elements of both corporations and partnerships. It offers limited liability protection to the owners of the business while providing the flexibility of a partnership when it comes to managing the taxation and management of the company.
- **Nonprofit Corporation:** in this type of business, the generation of profit and revenue is not the primary concern for the owners, and the main concern is inclined toward pursuing charitable, educational, or religious objectives.
- **Cooperative:** It is owned and controlled by its members, who could be customers, employees, or producers. The primary concern is to generate profit and distribute it among its members.

Apart from the corporate structure, the business model of a new venture should also include projected startup costs and financing sources, the company's target customer base, marketing strategy, a competitive analysis, and revenue and expense projections. The strategy may also include opportunities for the company to collaborate with other well-established businesses. For example, an advertising company's business model may identify benefits from a referral arrangement with a printing company.

Successful business models deliver a product at a competitive price and a sustainable cost. Many businesses revise their business models over time in order to better reflect changing business environments and demands.

When assessing a company as a potential investment, the investor should learn how it makes money. This entails scrutinizing the company's business model. To be honest, the business model may not reveal everything about a company's prospects. However, an investor who understands the business model can make better sense of the financial data.

Evaluating the Success of Business Models

Many businesses make the mistake of underestimating the costs of funding the business until it becomes profitable when developing their business models. Counting the costs of a product's launch is insufficient. A business must continue to operate until its revenues exceed its expenses.

The gross profit of a company is one of several ways analysts and investors evaluate the success of a business model. The gross profit of a business is total revenue minus the cost of sales. When a company's gross profit is compared to that of its main competitor or industry, it reveals the efficiency and effectiveness of its business model. However, gross profit alone can be quite deceptive. Analysts are also interested in cash flow and net income, which indicates how much real profit the company generates.

Pricing and costs are the two main levers of a company's business model. A business can raise prices and find inventory at a lower cost. Gross profit is increased by both actions. Many analysts believe that gross profit is more important when assessing a business plan. A healthy gross profit indicates a sound business strategy.

Types of Business Models

There are as many different types of business models as there are different types of businesses. Traditional business models include direct sales, franchising, advertising-based businesses, and brick-and-mortar stores. There are also hybrid models, such as businesses that combine internet retail with physical stores or with sporting organizations such as the NBA.

The following are some examples of common business models; keep in mind that the examples may fall into multiple categories.

Retailer

The retailer model is one of the most common business models that most people are familiar with. A retailer is the final link in the supply chain. They frequently purchase finished goods from manufacturers or distributors and deal directly with customers.

Manufacturer

A manufacturer is in charge of obtaining raw materials and completing products using internal labor, machinery, and equipment. A manufacturer may create custom items or mass-produced items that are highly replicated. A manufacturer can also sell to distributors, retailers, or customers directly.

Freemium

Customers are drawn to freemium business models because they are introduced to basic, limited-scope products. The company then attempts to convert the client to a more premium, advanced product that requires payment while the client is using their service. Although a customer can theoretically remain on freemium indefinitely, a company tries to demonstrate the benefits of becoming an upgraded member.

Ultimately, the business model choice is between adopting or taking a pattern from a known or proven model used by established firms and what is known in small business jargon as a disruptive model, which follows no existing models or combines elements of existing ones in novel ways.

A company is more than just a business that sells products. It is an ecosystem that requires a strategy for who to sell to, what to sell, how much to charge, and what value it creates. A business model describes what an organization does to create long-term value for its customers in a systematic manner. After developing a business model, a company should have a clearer idea of how it wants to operate and what its financial future looks like.

Let us now shed some light on the five components in Thompson's Business Model that are an integral part of any business:

i. **Business Mindset:** Whether you are in the early stages of your business or have years of expertise makes no difference. In order to be successful, you must have a business mindset.

Business owners contribute to economic development by creating jobs and developing products or services that improve the world. Being a successful entrepreneur necessitates thinking outside the box and having bold ideas. To succeed, one must be creative, communicative, and highly motivated while also remaining open to risk and failure.

Some important characteristics of a business mindset are:

Positive Mental Attitude

Successful entrepreneurs must maintain a positive attitude and outlook. The CEO's mindset sets the tone for the rest of the company and influences corporate culture.

Negative thoughts hinder progress and the ability of management to lead and motivate employees. Therefore, in order to attain business success, one must adopt a positive outlook, as this positivity helps entrepreneurs weather business downturns.

Persuasive Communication Ability

The most successful entrepreneurs are persuasive people. Persuasion can help you negotiate a better price for your inventory. Not to mention that persuasive people tend to be inspiring leaders, which makes them excellent bosses.

Persuasive communication skills can be learned and practiced, even though some people are more naturally persuasive than others. Learning to communicate and present your ideas will help you become a better entrepreneur, regardless of your industry.

Stop the Blame Game

In order to be a successful business owner, you must learn to take accountability for whatever goes wrong because, at the end of the day, it's *your* company, and you are responsible for it. Blaming others when things go sideways does nothing but create negativity and, perhaps, a toxic environment in the workplace. So, let go of the negativity, stop blaming others, and instead focus your energy on finding a solution.

ii. **Revenue Model:** Revenue models should not be confused with pricing models, which are used by businesses to determine the best possible price for what they are selling in order to maximize profits. Once the pricing strategy has been determined, the revenue model will govern how customers pay that price when they make a purchase.

Pricing models are used by RevOps teams to forecast revenue for future business planning. Knowing where your cash is coming from and how you'll get it helps predict how frequently it will arrive.

There are various revenue models that businesses use, and we will cover some below:

Advertising Revenue Model

Selling advertising space to other businesses is a component of the advertising revenue model. This space is desired because the advertiser (who is selling the space) has high traffic and large audiences that the buyer (who is purchasing the space) wants to take advantage of in order to increase the visibility of their business, product, or service.

Sales Revenue Model

According to the sales revenue model, you make money by selling goods and services to customers both online and in person. As a result, any business that sells products and services directly employs this model.

For example, clothing stores that only sell their products through a storefront or a business-specific retail website use the sales revenue model because they sell directly to consumers without the involvement of a third party.

iii. **Gross Margin:** Gross Margin measures profit as a percentage of sales revenue and is a good yardstick for measuring how efficiently companies make money from products and services. As a result, it can be used to compare companies with varying sales revenues more easily.

Gross profit margin focuses on sales revenue as well as general corporate expenses and other costs and income that affect a company's overall profitability, such as legal settlements or interest income.

The gross profit margin is sometimes used to assess how well a company is managed. High gross profit margins indicate that management is efficient at generating revenue based on the labor and other costs associated with producing its products and services.

Large changes in gross profit margin from quarter to quarter or year to year can sometimes indicate poor management. Other issues that could cause fluctuations in gross profit margin include temporary manufacturing issues that result in lower product quality and a higher level of product returns, lowering net sales revenue.

A company's goal is to have a high gross profit margin. A high gross profit margin not only drives more profit to the bottom line but also leaves more money to invest in research and development.

The definition of a healthy gross profit margin varies depending on the industry. A startup or relatively new business may have a lower gross profit margin than more established industry peers because it may offer significant discounts to gain market share and cannot yet benefit from the economies of scale enjoyed by larger companies.

iv. Operating Model: An operating model is a graphical representation of how a company provides value to both internal and external customers.

Operating models, also known as value-chain maps, are developed to assist employees in visualizing and comprehending the role that each function of an organization plays in meeting the needs of others.

Operating models are useful resources for helping managers understand how a change in dynamics in one part of the organization may affect the value delivered by other parts. They are typically organized from the top down and can be extremely high-level or extremely granular.

A large organization may require the development of dozens of operating models to accurately capture the steps that each department must take in order to successfully meet the needs of other parts of the business and customers.

v. Attracting Financing: A majority of people who have started businesses in this day and age do not fit the traditional stereotype of a business owner. Business owners now come from diverse backgrounds. In the recent past, more and more entrepreneurs are people who identify as females, senior citizens, and people from racially diverse communities. People have been instilled with the confidence and trust that if they work hard on their passions, their dream of scaling their small business will one day come true.

Seeing that adequate initial investment is crucial for any startup to survive in the market, many businesses turn toward angel investors and venture capitalists to raise funds. However, only a small percentage of businesses ever receive venture capital funding.

Fortunately, there are numerous other ways to generate cash flow for your business. For example, instead of relying solely on venture capital, business owners can focus their skills on creating value. You can still grow your business by being creative, thinking outside the box, and allocating your time and money wisely.

One of the key metrics for a company's health is how much cash it can generate. Let's look at some innovative ways to get funding and resources for your business:

Embrace Social Media And Digital Marketing

Social media is one of the best and cheapest ways to get noticed. TikTok, one of the fastest-growing platforms available today, for example, offers business owners numerous opportunities to connect with leads and drive sales. Best of all, you can do much of the work yourself by making simple and entertaining videos.

Finding Alternative Funding

Finally, think about other possible funding sources. Venture capital may be out of your price range, but a small business loan could provide you with the funds you need to grow your company. A small business loan with a cheaper interest rate, for example, could provide you with the capital you need to open a second location. This option might turn out to be far more beneficial when compared with venture capital, who can sometimes seek equity upfront to invest in your company.

Of all the business models on offer, companies should opt for one that suits their necessities and provides them the groundwork for consistent profitability and expansion.

Not every industry is suited to every business model. Furthermore, each business model is unique. Consider the shaving business. Gillette is content to sell its Mach3 razor handle at cost or below in order to attract repeat customers for its more profitable razor blades.

To get those blade sales, the business model relies on selling the handle as a standalone and then selling razors at a premium since these will be required on a weekly/monthly basis. This variation on the broader freemium business model is now known as the razor-razorblade model; however, it can also apply to any company that sells a product at a deep discount in order to supply a dependent good at a significantly higher price.

The bottom line is to select the business model that best fits the products or services you provide. If you understand the five components of Thompson & Company's business model, the road to success will be a smooth path for you.

Chapter 4: Direct Sales

Direct selling is selling products in a non-retail setting, such as at home, online, or other locations other than a store. It eliminates distribution middlemen such as wholesalers and regional distribution centers. Products are delivered directly from the manufacturer to the sales company, then to the sales rep or distributor, and finally to the consumer.

Direct sales products are not typically found in traditional retail locations. This means that the only way to obtain them is through a distributor or representative.

Direct selling is commonly associated with party plan and network marketing companies. However, they aren't the only ones who utilize direct sales. Many B2B companies target and sell to their end customers through direct selling. For example, many companies that sell office supplies will send representatives directly to stores that can benefit from their services.

It is critical to understand that direct selling is not the same as direct marketing. In the case of the former, individual distributors or representatives contact customers directly. In direct marketing, however, a company markets directly to customers. Emails, flyers, promotional letters, outdoor advertising, ads, phone calls, and websites are some examples of direct marketing.

Types of Direct Selling

There is a myriad of ways business owners can utilize direct selling, including:

- **Single-level Direct Sales:** This type of direct selling is typically done in person, such as through door-to-door or one-on-one presentations. It can, however, take place online. As a result, salespeople are compensated through commission sales and occasional bonuses from the company where they obtain their products. They do not hire additional sales representatives in order to increase their earnings.

- **Host or Party-plan Sales:** Sales of this nature typically occur in a gathering of people. Hosting a party where things can be purchased is the most effective way to generate interest in your company's services. Salespeople employ the party-plan sales technique to generate repeat sales by inquiring customers whether or not they would be interested in hosting their own selling parties. Mary Kay is a classic example of direct selling because its representatives frequently hold parties to promote the company's products and recruit new representatives. Tupperware is also a great example of a party-plan company that approaches homemakers to host product demonstrations in their homes. Representatives give a demonstration of the product to the attendees, and the host is compensated with a commission.

- **Multi-level Marketing (MLM):** Multi-level Marketing, also known as network marketing, is a direct selling strategy in which products or services are sold directly to consumers through independent sales representatives rather than employees of the company. A multi-level marketer's primary goal isn't to sell products but rather to recruit new team members. MLM is distinct from other forms of direct selling in that its participants earn money through commissions on their own sales and the sales of new business partners they bring into the fold.

People who wish to earn money from home often join multi-level marketing companies (MLMs). However, doing so can be risky owing to the high startup costs, strict requirements, and compensation structure that sometimes depend on the number of people one recruits. For these reasons, multi-level marketing schemes are rarely viewed favorably.

Direct Selling Techniques

There are many different direct selling techniques, but some of the most popular ones are listed below:

- **FAB (Features – Advantages – Benefits):** This scheme is used in most scripts, landing pages, and promotional materials. It entails consistently informing customers about a company's or product's key features, main benefits, and positive effects on a prospect. This technique clarifies an offer for a consumer and increases their interest.

- **BYAF (But You Are Free):** Persistence is essential for closing deals, but salespeople risk overdoing it. As a result, customers are often turned off by pushy brand representatives after just one purchase. Allowing customers to make their own choices during negotiations is a great way to obtain new customers and retain old ones.

- **The Foot-in-the-Door Strategy:** The core idea of this upselling technique is to make small initial requests followed by larger ones. Another option is to start with a low price and then charge more for more comprehensive services, i.e., placing your foot in the door with an initial attractive offer and then continuously widening the crack with relatively more expensive services. For example, if you are selling online English lessons to international students, you could start with a lower-cost level 1 course and then negotiate the purchase of the entire expensive course with the customer.

- **SPIN Marketing:** People like to feel that they are in control of a conversation or a negotiation. Take advantage of this tendency by employing the SPIN technique. Allow a customer to speak more than yourself during negotiations, and ask them questions about their situation (S), problem (P), implication (I), and the need for a solution (N, or need-payoff). After going through all the stages, you can introduce your product as the key to resolving the prospective customer's problems.

- **The Preferential Approach:** Humans, as social beings, usually give something in return for the favors they receive. This characteristic is central to the widely used reciprocity principle. To encourage reciprocity, offer something in advance, such as a free trial period, a discount, or an additional service to your customer. This goodwill gesture will persuade the customer to accept your offer.

Advantages of Direct Sales

It is always pertinent to look at the Direct Sales Model from the perspective of your business and then proceed to apply any strategy. Here are some of the Direct Sales Model's advantages that may be worthwhile to consider:

- **Coordination with Other Business Strategies:** A direct sales approach gives a small firm more leeway in coordinating sales interactions with manufacturing and marketing objectives because the small business owns its sales team. The company may make sure that its salespeople who deal directly with clients utilize the same marketing language and techniques as its media ads. To put it another way, this helps drive home marketing messaging to consumers. Small businesses can learn a lot about their customers' wants and needs through direct sales. The information they glean from these conversations can be used to improve future marketing efforts and product development.

- **Cost and Price Control:** A small business adopting the direct sales model has a substantial degree of control over its price and distribution. As a result, the corporation has increased the capability to verify that its items are competitively priced. The firm can also verify that the individuals representing its products or services are knowledgeable and effective. Additionally, a direct sales model firm has reduced reliance on merchants. According to studies published in Management Science, this part of the model can help a small firm negotiate better terms with a retailer, giving it a better shot at keeping a greater slice of the profit pie.

- **Access to More Customers:** A direct selling strategy provides small businesses access to consumers it may not have been able to reach otherwise. Not all clients receive or respond to media advertising initiatives. Similarly, some clients may not shop at the retail establishments that offer a business's items. The direct sales approach is a means to get to these people directly and begin a deal. A direct sales strategy where a small business makes use of pre-existing social connections is not uncommon. In these instances, the sales staff is urged to market primarily to their friends and family. It is crucial to recall some clients are put off by this approach; therefore, it should be followed with a degree of sensitivity.

Disadvantages of Direct Selling

While direct selling has many advantages, it also has some disadvantages, some of which include:

- **Creating Networks:** For sales reps or distributors, direct selling can be a tricky scheme. Generally, the manufacturing company does not provide any leads. As a result, sales reps must forge their own network.

- **Chances of Developing a Pyramid Scheme:** A pyramid scheme is a fraudulent business model in which the initial promoters recruit investors who are required to pay an upfront fee to take part in the business. They are then required to recruit more investors to get returns. If the seller/manufacturer focuses on incentivizing sales reps to recruit new people rather than selling products, a pyramid scheme may form.

- **Not Always a Simple Approach:** When it comes to business growth or expansion, direct selling can be a difficult method to employ. This business model relies heavily on distributors and sales representatives. Furthermore, this business model will only work if your reps/distributors provide consistent and growing sales.

- **Excellent Marketing Skills Necessary:** Finally, persuading a customer and selling a product door-to-door is extremely difficult, so direct selling requires reps and distributors to have "impeccable" marketing skills.

Direct Selling vs. Pyramid Schemes

Due to their similarities, it can be difficult to differentiate between a pyramid scheme and a legitimate multi-level marketing business opportunity. Participants (called "distributors") in both MLM and pyramid schemes are rewarded based on the number of new recruits they bring in, making the two business models quite similar. The key distinction is that distributors' payments in pyramid schemes are meant to be perpetual.

Distributors in a pyramid scheme would typically be expected to pay fees and stock up on items they won't need in order to maintain the scheme's revenue stream. The firm cares more about maintaining a regular supply of cash from distributors than it does about the people who sell its products or services. So, most participants' income rests heavily on how effectively they recruit. Indicators of a possible pyramid scheme include the following:

- Exaggerated claims of overnight success
- Putting in too much effort to find new wholesalers
- A request for a significant sum at the outset
- Marketer's emotional appeal to sign up for their service
- The product itself is either not mentioned or not highlighted enough.

Starting a Direct Sales Company

Starting a direct sales company provides control over the amount of work that is accomplished and the time that is spent.

Some benefits of a Direct Sales company include:

- **Low Starting Costs:** Unlike other franchise companies, there isn't a need to pay large fees to get started as an independent contractor. The majority of the initial costs are spent on inventory, which can be recouped after selling the product to clients.

- **Schedules Can be Adjusted:** A personalized schedule can be set, and items can be sold whenever it is most convenient because the business can be operated from anywhere.

- **Opportunities Available for Advancement and Training:** If a reputed marketing company is chosen, training and learning opportunities are provided to help improve sales and marketing skills, resulting in opportunities to earn a higher income.

Determining Niche

Considering products that will improve customer's lives before committing to selling them is extremely important. Researching companies providing similar products once a settled market or a niche is decided is the essential first step. It is also prudent to find out if the company in question is worth the time and effort by researching it online and analyzing reviews written by customers and employees. It is also smart to find a product that will improve and have some sort of impact on the lives of the target audience.

Conclusion

Direct selling is an alternative to traditional employment for those looking for a flexible way to supplement household income or whose circumstances prevent them from working full-time. Direct selling opportunities can lead to a rewarding career for those who succeed and choose to pursue their independent direct selling business full-time. Direct selling typically has low startup costs. A low-cost sales kit is usually all that is required to get started, with little or no inventory or other cash outlay required to get started. This contrasts with the cost and risk associated with larger outlays in other businesses.

Direct selling provides a distribution channel for businesses with innovative or distinctive products that are not suitable for other retailing due to cost or other factors.

Direct selling positively benefits the economies and people where direct selling companies operate and provides consumers with a convenient source of quality products.

Chapter 5: Franchise Model

The business franchise model, also known as franchising, is a legal agreement. An established brand (franchisor) allows an independent business owner (franchisee) to use its procedures, technical know-how, brand name, reputation, branding, and intellectual property in this business model. In exchange, the franchisee pays a fee and follows the rules and regulations outlined in the agreement. Thus, franchising is the sharing of a brand between two businesses. As a result, regardless of where the customer goes, the product or service is the same.

If we take a look back in time, some three hundred years ago, it was indeed Benjamin Franklin who entered into the first franchise agreement with Thomas Whitmarsh in 1731 to supply printing services in Charlestown, South Carolina, and is thought to be the founder of modern franchising. Isaac M. Singer revisited the franchising strategy to distribute Singer sewing machines in the early 1850s. Due to Ray Kroc's invention of the McDonald's hamburger stand, franchising did not become popular until a century after Singer.

The business model of franchising is not novel. In reality, franchising stretches back to the Middle Ages and ancient China. During the Middle Ages, the local landowner would offer the peasants or serfs permission to hunt, organize markets or fairs, or conduct other business in his domain, likely for a fee. With these new opportunities of doing business came regulations, and these rules were incorporated into the European Common Law.

During the 1920s and 1930s, the franchising model was widely utilized in the restaurant industry. New physical communication networks (such as the Interstate Highway System in the United States) enabled people to travel long distances in their cars.

The success story of McDonald's restaurants all over the world is deeply ingrained in the franchise model. In the 1960s, the now multi-billion dollar food chain began experimenting and applying a franchising model to grow its restaurant business, and it grew into a restaurant behemoth over the 1960s.

McDonald's capitalized on the existing "Speedy Service System" developed by the McDonald's brothers (what we would later refer to as "fast food"), which was an incredible process development capable of providing an improved product at a faster pace. The rapid system exemplified the application of the manufacturing process to the restaurant industry and brought about rapid changes across the board, with several companies adopting the same strategies to increase growth and efficiencies in their restaurant chains.

There are currently thousands of franchises in hundreds of businesses and markets. According to a 2018 government report, the franchise business employed 21 million people and created $2.3 trillion in economic activity.[2] The power of franchising is that independent businesses share a brand, resulting in tremendous growth and wealth creation.

The following are examples of common franchise agreements:

Business Format Franchise

This is one of the most common franchise agreements, in which the franchisor grants the franchisee the right to utilize the franchisor's business model and trademarks in exchange for an initial franchise fee and a continuing portion of sales. In addition, franchisees follow all policies established by the leading firm.

Product Distribution Franchise

In the product distribution franchise model, the franchisor produces the product while the franchisee sells it. With a few exceptions, this connection is comparable to the supplier-dealer relationship. Under this franchise arrangement, the franchisee

---

[2] https://www.inspiringtrend.com/franchising-is-a-very-convenient-way-to-spread-ones-business-nation-or-worldwide/

may distribute the items on an exclusive or semi-exclusive basis, whereas in the supplier-dealer partnership, the dealer may offer multiple brands simultaneously. Coca-Cola, John Deere, and the Ford Motor Company are examples of product distribution franchises.

Manufacturing Franchise

In this agreement, the franchisee has the exclusive right to manufacture and distribute the parent company's products under its trade name and trademark.

Types of Franchise Ownership

Single-unit Franchisee: A franchisee is called a single-unit franchisee when they purchase their first franchise. This is the most prevalent franchise ownership structure.

Multi-unit Franchisee: If a franchisee is successful with their first franchise, they may decide to launch multiple franchises with the same franchisor. When a franchisee owns many franchise units, they are known as multi-unit owners.

Multi-unit Area Development: This strategy is optimal for franchisees who desire market exclusivity and have the means to negotiate it with the franchisor.

Master Franchisee: A master franchisee is comparable to a multi-unit area developer in that they are committed to opening a particular number of sites within a certain time frame and geographical area. The master franchisee has the ability and sometimes the obligation to sell franchises to other potential franchisees. The master franchisee acts as an intermediary between the franchisee and the franchisor.

Subway's Business Model

Subway's business model is centered on its franchise-only structure and non-traditional locations. Through this model, franchisees can open many stores worldwide, create brand awareness, and reach the masses. This also helps keep expenses low and profits high, which allows them to remain price-competitive when selling franchises to potential customers. Most of Subway's development and growth in revenue can be attributed to this model as it promotes motivation among its owners and builds more trust in the tried and tested Franchise Model. As a result, Subway continues to use a 100% franchise model to this day.

Motivating Franchisees

Subway encourages franchisees to strive for excellence by presenting the 'Franchisee of the Year' and 'Development Agent of the Year' awards at their annual conferences. These awards highlight the efforts and achievements of franchisees, such as opening new stores, boosting sales and profits, and receiving outstanding store ratings.

Additionally, franchisees are supplied with business management guidance. Subway Development Agents are essential to the continued growth of the Subway brand in their territories.

Non-traditional Units

Daring to enter non-traditional markets is also an important aspect of Subway's business strategy. They can examine the country's economic impact and future growth by developing a proprietary model. This enables them to plan and optimize their franchises in areas where they can have many restaurants and create a faster economic impact.

Attempting to branch out and innovate, one of their franchisees was creative and opened his store in a convenience store, which many thought was impossible and odd. However, this step enabled Subway to capitalize on low entry costs while profiting from the enormous number of convenience outlets across the country. As a result, by merging both franchising and non-traditional units, companies can break out from the conventional and capitalize on new prospects.

Furthermore, non-traditional stores (such as airports, transit hubs, and Walmart) enable franchisees to reach more people. These are folks who may not have considered Subway as an option before. This aids in increasing brand awareness and expanding commercial opportunities.

The Cost of Franchising a Subway Restaurant

The inexpensive cost of starting a franchise is one of the main selling points for Subway. The franchisee is normally required to pick a store location and pay the startup expenditures as the first stage in starting a franchise enterprise. The initial costs for a retail location include real estate and construction charges. The overall cost of the initial restaurant location for a Subway business is projected to be between $116,000 and $243,000, which is significantly less than the cost of rival fast food franchises.

Other expenses are associated with franchising the business. A $15,000 startup licensing price is required to launch the firm, compared to a $40,000 to $90,000 licensing fee for Dunkin' (DNKN) or a $45,000 fee for McDonald's (MCD).

Royalty fees are also required on an annual basis. Subway charges a royalty fee of 8% of annual gross sales, which is greater than the 5% and 4% charged by Dunkin' Donuts and McDonald's, respectively. In addition, the franchisee must pay an ad fund fee of 4.5% of total gross sales.[3]

Pros and Cons of a Franchise Business Model

There are numerous pros and cons to investing in a franchise. Among the widely acknowledged benefits is a ready-made business model. A franchise includes market-tested products and services and, in many cases, a well-known brand. If you are a McDonald's franchisee, decisions have already been made about the products you sell, the layout of your restaurant, and even the design of your employees' uniforms. Some franchisors even provide training, financial planning, and approved-supplier lists. However, even though franchises have a proven formula and track record, success is never assured.

There are substantial start-up expenses and recurring royalty fees. Continuing with the McDonald's example, the projected cost to launch a McDonald's franchise ranges between $1 million and $2.2 million.

By definition, franchises require recurring fees as a percentage of sales or revenue to be paid to the

---

[3] https://www.investopedia.com/articles/forex-currencies/081316/cost-buying-subway-franchise.asp

franchisor. This percentage can range from 4.6% to 12.5%, depending on the industry.

One of the major disadvantages of becoming a franchisee is erroneous information, which makes unverifiable claims regarding ratings, rankings, and accolades for emerging brands and businesses. This leads to franchisees spending high dollar amounts for a business with no or minimal value. Additionally, franchisees lack control over territory and business inventiveness.

Finally, financing from the franchisor or other sources may also be challenging. Other problems affecting all franchisees, such as poor location or management, are also possible.[4]

Franchisor and Franchisee Relationship

The franchisor is the parent firm that sells potential franchisees the rights to franchise its brand. The franchisor is responsible for developing the business, brand, and operational systems. The franchisor grants franchisees the rights to their proven business model, identifiable trademark, established business procedures, and training and support upon deciding to franchise their business.

---

[4] https://www.investopedia.com/articles/forex-currencies/081316/cost-buying-subway-franchise.asp

The franchisee is the individual who purchases the right to sell the items or services and use the above-mentioned established and proven business procedures. Although the franchisee is, in essence, purchasing an already-established firm, franchisees must work hard to gain market loyalty, attract talent, and expand the franchise business. Ultimately, the franchisee manages the day-to-day operations of the firm.

The franchisor-franchisee relationship should be based on mutual respect, appreciation, and assistance. Obviously, as is the case with all partnerships, no two are identical. Although franchisee-franchisor partnerships vary from brand to brand, one thing remains constant: the relationship is extremely important for both parties in the long run.

Franchisor Expectations

- **The FDD:** When a franchisee is sincere about a franchise opportunity, the franchisor will provide them with their Franchise Disclosure Document (FDD), which contains vital information concerning bankruptcies, various fees, franchisee obligations, and more.

- **Finance Alternatives:** Some franchisors offer financing services that assist franchisees in locating a loan servicer or other payment ways.

- **Location Services:** If the franchise requires a physical location, the franchisor will typically assist with site selection and locating a local contractor to build the approved architecture.

- **Instruction and Operational Direction:** In addition to an operational manual and in-person or online training, franchisors give franchisees information on how the firm operates. The operational handbook details all personnel positions, performance expectations, management procedures, and other criteria. Training typically occurs at the franchisor's corporate headquarters or through a combination of online and in-person training.

- **Marketing and Advertising:** Franchisors provide franchisees with marketing and promotion. This may be accomplished by television and radio advertisements or social media and email campaigns. Typically, franchisees are charged a marketing fee to compensate for this expense. Some franchisors provide additional services, such as administration, HR, and accounting, to their franchisees.

- **Support:** As the franchisee gets their business up and running, questions and concerns eventually arise. Throughout the franchise agreement, the franchisor will give varying levels of support. In addition, franchisees have access to a vast network of other franchisees who may be able to provide advice or a tried and tested solution to a common problem.

Licensing vs. Franchising

Understanding the distinction between franchising and licensing is a major source of confusion for potential franchisees. License is a broad phrase used for contracting reasons by enterprises. A license permits the licensee to collaborate with a brand, granting them access to its intellectual property, brand, design, and business programs. In exchange, the licensee pays the licensor royalties. The licensor may have input on how the intellectual property is utilized but not how the licensee does business. A licensor permits a licensee the right to use their intellectual property but does not provide assistance, training, or exercise control over how the licensee utilizes that intellectual property.

On the other hand, a franchise is a legal and commercial partnership between the owner of a firm (the franchisor) and an individual (the franchisee) who is launching a branch of that business using the trademark logos and business model of the franchisor. A franchise is essentially an independent branch of the franchise corporation while the franchisee sells the goods or services supplied by the franchisor.

Franchise Opportunity Vs. Business Opportunity

Another typical source of confusion is the distinction between franchise and business opportunities. While they may sound fairly similar at first, there are significant variations between them. For instance, a franchise opportunity includes the licensing of trademark rights, provides extensive training and operational assistance for the duration of the contract, and typically costs more than a business opportunity owing to recurring fees.

Although all business possibilities are unique and difficult to define, the primary distinction is that when pursuing a business opportunity, a person is unlikely to receive the same support, training, and direction as a franchisee from their franchisor.

Franchise Basics and Regulations

Franchise agreements are intricate and vary per franchisor. Typically, a franchise agreement will provide three payment types to the franchisor. Initially, the franchisee must pay an upfront fee to the franchisor for the managed rights or trademark. Second, the franchisor is frequently compensated for training, equipment, and business consulting services. The franchisor also receives ongoing royalties or a percentage of the business's sales.

A franchise agreement is similar to a lease or rental agreement for a business. It does not imply that the franchisee owns the firm. Depending on the deal, franchise agreements normally last between five and thirty years, and franchisees who violate or dissolve the contract prematurely face severe fines.

Franchises are regulated at the state level in the United States. In 1979, however, the Federal Trade Commission (FTC) enacted federal regulation. The Franchise Rule is a legal disclosure that franchisors must provide to potential purchasers. The franchisor must communicate all risks, advantages, and restrictions associated with a franchise investment. This data includes fees and expenses, litigation history, approved business vendors or suppliers, estimated financial performance objectives, and other pertinent information. Formerly known as the Uniform Franchise Offering Circular, this disclosure requirement was renamed the Franchise Disclosure Document in 2007.

Conclusion

Globally, it has been observed that in reaction to the COVID-19 pandemic, franchise firms were able to make more rapid adjustments than traditional businesses. Franchisors moved swiftly by implementing changes to their business and marketing strategies all at once, notwithstanding the multi-city nature of their operations.

In the post-pandemic era, we have observed the constant growth of established enterprises and the emergence of new franchises in categories such as

Restaurants, Lifestyles, Wellness, Health Aids, and other Services.

Post-pandemic, the franchise business model has proved to be the leading employment generator with rapid business openings, faster hiring, and more stable performance than independent businesses. The pandemic also made us understand that franchise business models have the potential to resolve challenges through agile shifts in business operations and become a source of stability in a volatile economic landscape.

Chapter 6: Freemium Model

The 1980s witnessed a boom in the tech sector, where organizations and business corporations massively integrated their business operations with computer technology. Particularly the software companies, for which this has been a necessary practice in order to sustain growth. Thus, laying the foundations of the Freemium business model.

Software developing companies started offering their products with basic features that had limited-service offerings. Then, in order for customers to have a fully enhanced experience of their digital products, they had to acquire a full package or the upgrade at a price. This eventually became a popular business model for game-developing companies as well. For example, game developers welcome their audience to play their games for free, but they can only unlock their special features, add-ons, plug-ins, or advanced levels by paying a specific amount or a regular subscription.

As the timeline transitioned into the 21st century, the conventional wisdom on freemium business models experienced immense optimization. It started with the giants prevailing in the world, such as Facebook and Google. They're best known for providing their free products, offering their selling points at a premium rate.

The Freemium Business Model

As of yet, you might've already guessed the mechanism behind a freemium business model. A freemium business model provides initial services to its customers free of cost in an attempt to derive demand for future transactions. Through the provision of services at a basic level without even imposing costs to the consumer, entities establish a relationship with their customer base, eventually offering them advanced services in the future, such as add-ons, enhanced storage, unlimited usage limit, or maybe an add-free experience.

Plenty of new business ventures nowadays are seeking to adopt a freemium business model in order to get in the game. However, there exists a lot of misconceptions as to what a freemium model may entail for businesses. Newbie entrepreneurs should understand that freemium products are not the same as offering premium products with a free sample. There is a considerable amount of software companies that provide their users with a free option but with the prime objective of having the majority of users pay for their services.

Not for everyone

It should be made clear that not all products or services are compatible with being developed under a freemium business model. This model appeals to many startups as they're able to capture the attention of many of their prospects in a short time span. They tell themselves that they can have a business model that can supplement them enough money to cover their initial costs and that they could break even in a shorter period before they actually start earning profit.

How does a freemium business model work?

Phil Libin, Founder and CEO of Evernote, manages an entity running on a freemium business model. He has given his insights as to how entrepreneurs can structure their businesses with this model. He has detailed four key steps for operating a successful freemium business model:

Acquire an adequate number of free users: Though the strategy may seem obvious, it is an important point to consider. A freemium business is dependent upon the science of numbers. For example, if your business projects that only 3 percent of your users are going to use your free subscription, then in order to complete a sales target of $100,000, you need to lure in a lot of customers enough to pay that targeted sales amount.

Maintaining your user base: Only acquiring these customers is not enough; businesses have to work on a lot of strategies that can help them maintain their customer base in the long run.

Develop a product or service: Developing a product or service, the value of which increases over time, is the most important principle in the freemium business model. It also goes along for other businesses in general. Your business needs to consistently build the value of its products so that more and more people flock under your brand's umbrella.

Minimize your costs: As cliché as it may sound, this is particularly true for all freemium businesses. Under this business model, the seller incurs a lower marginal cost for each user. Therefore, you have to maintain a fairly low operational cost. This is known as 'internet economics' as there are abundant open source and cloud computing services that help in reducing costs.

Key Considerations Before Opting for a Freemium Business Model

It is important to determine whether a freemium business model would be a viable growth tool for your business. Let us examine these determinants:

Resources

Does the entity have an appropriate set of resources that can supplement a better-functioning freemium model? Most may tend to undermine the importance of the upkeep of a free resource. If we take an example of freemium digital software, it would require the developer to have overwatch on multiple matters, i.e., maintenance, updates, back-end support, or anything else. If your business doesn't ensure these things, your product might be an eventual flop.

Free vs. Premium

Is there a possibility that your free product is cannibalizing your premium offering? As we know, developing a freemium product is not a piece of cake; it is necessary to ensure that the basic features of your freemium product are offered at value– this means that you consider achieving a balance between what you may offer for free, and what may only have restricted access.

Business Strategy

Your organization's objectives are necessary constituents to ensure the success of your business model. For example, if the entity has its foundation structured on a sales team, opting for a freemium model is a considerate choice that would make it possible for your organization to lure in more people. However, you can ask yourself if your freemium model will be able to acquire more potential enterprise customers through its customer base. If not, then your freemium model may not be aligned with your overall business strategy.

Making the Right Choice

Let's just say that your entity has developed a digital product that has 15 features embedded, and you have made available five features free for anyone who registers for your product.

Therefore, users who want to experience the other ten features would have to pay. However, it all comes back to our burning question: how would you know whether you've made the right choices? How can you know that the customers would be motivated to pay for the premium features?

One of the key features of freemium products is to attract new customers. If your business is having a problem succeeding with that objective, it could mean that your service doesn't offer that appeal or isn't compelling enough to attract an audience. You may need to provide more features or enhance the quality.

However, if you're still able to capture abundant traffic but only a handful of customers are willing to pay for your service, you might have the opposite problem.

This could be a possibility as your basic offerings are too generous such that people aren't willing to pay for the additional services.

New York Times, an American daily newspaper, has been familiarized with the same problem. For a couple of years, the newspaper was available to the public with unrestricted access. In 2011, the newspaper began restricting access to customers with 20 free articles per month.

Therefore, people started subscribing to the broadsheet for a complete experience.

Gradually, the company learned that it was gathering a very low number of subscribers than what they expected. Therefore, they had to bring the number down to ten free articles per month.

This tells us that developers should work on finding the optimum balance between traffic and paying the customers. In practice, this might be a challenging strategy as users would be required to pay for features that were available to them for free.

Key Metrics for Measuring Success

In order to measure the success of your freemium model, there are certain benchmarks against which you can compare your business success. You can have a look at these key metrics and use them against your business for an effective critical analysis of your business model.

- **Total cost divided by the number of current users**

- The rate at which basic users apply for premium services.

- **Daily Active User (DAU)**; this feature is used to show the number of people currently engaged with your product or service. For other platforms, you can use slightly different metrics, such as monthly active users. It depends upon the time frame in which you're looking to measure success.

- **Average Revenue per User (ARPU);** the total number of subscription earnings divided by the total number of current users.

- **Average Revenue Per Daily Active Use (ARPDU);** the total number of earnings divided by the total number of Active Users.

- **Average Revenue Per Paying User (ARPPU);** the total number of earnings divided by the total number of users subscribed to your premium service.

- **Lifetime Value (LTV)**

- **Daily Sessions;** the number of sessions each day in which a user interacts with your product.

- **CPA: Cost Per Acquisition or Cost**

Pros and Cons of Freemium Business

It could be established by learning the Freemium model that this business structure seems effective for technology startups— this is because they are in the initial stages of their business cycle, and their core strategies would be established around building a sufficient following for their product. Freemium models are widely recognized for bringing abundant brand awareness at the initial stages while not feeling the need to provide a lot of customer service. However, along with the benefits this model brings, there is also a flipside to this structure. You can assess both of these sides by examining the following points:

Advantages

- It provides a slightly more hassle-free way for businesses to acquire potential users and collect their information and data.
- They can generate revenue through online adverts and boost their business applications.
- For startups, it assists with a large amount of brand awareness without necessitating a lot of customer support.

Disadvantages

- No guarantee that free users will convert to paid users.

- There might be too many features provided on the product's basic version that may prevent the users from switching to the premium version.

- Users may be discouraged from using the basic version if it doesn't offer a good experience.

Examples of Businesses Operating Under a Freemium Model

Spotify

Spotify is one of the biggest businesses in the world that uses the freemium revenue model. It is a music-streaming app that has a free ad-supported tier and a variety of ad-free paid subscriptions. It's a perfect example of a business operating on a freemium model.

Back in 2015, the service received abundant criticism for its overreliance on its free tier. However, the company defended itself against the prevailing backlash and proved itself to be one of the fastest streaming services in the world. In 2019, it was the fastest streaming service documented to reach a hundred million paying users worldwide. It also currently has the highest ratio of paid to unpaid users – more than 1/3 of its subscribers pay for its service.

Skype

It's an application that allows users to make audio and video calls online. Skype is documented to have more than 600 million free users. Although there is only a small proportion of users that pay subscriptions to make regular phone calls, this particular customer segment accounts for more than one billion dollars in revenue.

LinkedIn

This professional service provides a platform for businesses and other organizations to recruit individuals and accompany other business applications actively. It is also one of the largest businesses working under the freemium model, with more than 500 million users registered to this service, with at least half of its users registered actively. Subscribers are not necessarily required to pay for anything, but some services are charged, such as ad-free experience for recruiters and companies.

Conclusion

Over the past decade, the combination of providing free and premium services by businesses has become a dominant practice in the tech industry. Particularly for internet startups and application developers, these companies have grown rather fond of it. However, considering the vast benefits it provides to the users, it isn't necessarily compatible with all types of business organizations. Even if your business is compliant with the freemium model, you are required to run your business in a certain manner, with the appropriate resources and strategies, and compare their performance with a pre-determined benchmark for making the model an eventual success.

Chapter 7: Subscription Model

Subscription models are utilized in nearly all industries today. Successfully growing companies such as Netflix, Dollar Shave Club, and Microsoft have utilized a subscription-based revenue model for years.

A subscription business model entails a recurring revenue structure in which clients pay a weekly, monthly, or annual fee for products or services. In addition, a customer's subscription can be easily renewed after an agreed-upon time without the hassle of paying through a dedicated payment channel. As a result, this model enables businesses to improve customer relationships by providing hassle-free service and generating a steady income stream.

How Does a Subscription Model Operate?

Clients are charged regularly for a product or service under a subscription model. However, they can decide how long they wish to receive the service, and most subscriptions allow them to renew or cancel at any time.

Consider a subscription to be an agreement between a service provider and the customer. The customer agrees to pay for a service on a recurring basis, and the business agrees to fulfill the agreement as long as the customer maintains their recurring payments. The customer can renew or annul their subscription when the contract expires.

Subscription-based revenue models are advantageous for both the business and the client. As a customer, you can automatically repurchase a product or service you will need in the future. As a business, you can retain customers for future sales rather than having to constantly re-engage them to stay with your company. This makes it possible to secure monthly recurring revenue (MRR), which can keep the revenue flowing even during the worst economic conditions.

The local newspaper is a good example of a subscription model. While newspapers can be purchased individually, most readers subscribe to a weekly or monthly arrangement. In this way, instead of visiting the store to purchase a newspaper, you pay a flat fee to have one delivered to your home.

Advantages of a Subscription-based Business Model

- **Subscription Models Are Convenient for Customers**: People have busy lives. They are more likely to sign up for a service if they can have a product delivered when they need it with minimal effort. Subscriptions eliminate the need for consumers to research and purchase new products in-store, resulting in a more streamlined customer experience.

- **Customers Can Learn About New Products**: Individuals save money by not having to physically visit the store and have the opportunity to try new products they may not have intended to purchase.

Take Snack Crate, for instance, where you can purchase international snack boxes with several delightful treats inside. With this subscription, a customer might discover a previously unknown favorite snack and order that in the future.

- **Businesses Can Forecast Revenue Accurately**: Subscription models make it much simpler to forecast a business's monthly revenue. Since customers make repeated payments, a service provider knows how much each payment will be—this accurately represents a company's resources and financial position when incorporating budget into a business strategy.

- **Subscriptions Can Increase the Number of Customers**: Occasionally, the price of a good or service may be prohibitive for a consumer. Charging on a weekly, monthly, or annual basis allows them the ease with which they can afford and pay for those goods and services.

Consider purchasing a car. If you do not buy it outright, you will likely be placed on a payment plan in which you make payments over time. This allows you to afford the car, even if you cannot afford the entire cost of it upfront.

- **Subscriptions Decrease Customer Acquisition Costs**: Instead of wasting resources engaging with potential customers who do not know or trust your brand, subscription-based businesses enable word-of-mouth marketing. This reduces marketing expenses and enables more customer referrals. Generally speaking, word-of-mouth marketing is more effective and less expensive than promotional advertising.

Building a Subscription Model

Now that we have discussed how the subscription model works and its advantages, let us explore how a business can go about creating a subscription model:

- **Determine If Your Company Would Benefit From Offering Subscriptions**: Determining whether offering subscriptions makes sense for your products and services is key before developing subscription packages for your business. Ask yourself, do you sell products that require continuous customer access? Examples of this would include software, ongoing services (such as consulting or content writing), and exclusive media. Or is it a physical item for which customers will require refills? Commonplace items, books, and snacks may qualify here. Proceed to step two once you have determined whether your products and services would benefit from a subscription model.

- **Establish a Business Objective for Your Subscription-based Enterprise**: When creating subscription packages and pricing tiers, the right objective will direct your actions. For example, are you more interested in attracting high-value clients such as enterprise businesses, or do you wish to expand your clientele among small businesses? You may also wish to increase sales for a particular product, increase revenue by a certain percentage, or retain more customers.

Depending on your objectives, you will select a pricing structure that will help you attract and retain clients. It will also aid in determining the appropriate wording for your website's content.

- **Choose a Pricing Strategy for Subscriptions**: You may choose a particular pricing strategy depending on the nature of your product and your goals when developing your subscription model. For example, if your objective is to sell more user seats, you can opt for a per-user pricing model that offers a subscription discount to businesses with more users.

What Types of Companies Use a Subscription Model?

The recurring nature of subscription revenue is what makes it so popular, even with businesses you wouldn't expect. As a result, businesses have introduced monthly subscription options for various products and services.

While almost any business could adapt its business model to fit the subscription business model, it is best suited to a few types of businesses:

- **Content Access: Video, Music, Books, and Membership Sites**: Companies that provide ongoing access to content, such as video, audio, or books, are excellent subscription candidates.

Netflix, Hulu, and HBO all offer high-quality entertainment at a low cost in the streaming-video realm. While your $8.99 monthly Netflix fee may seem insignificant, consumers who have been subscribers for five years or more have contributed more than $500 to Netflix's coffers.

Subscriptions are also popular for music and books. For music, Spotify, Apple Music, and Tidal have been ahead of the curve in anticipating customer demands and trends. In addition, Amazon provides an eBook subscription service, and Audible provides unlimited access to audiobooks as long as the customer is subscribed.

- **Services Such as SaaS, Utilities, Insurance, and Leasing**: Subscriptions are also a good fit for service businesses. Many software companies now offer their software as a subscription service (SaaS) rather than as a one-time purchase. It is trickier for developers to make changes and improvements to their products with more traditional one-time software sales, relying on clunky system updates to deliver those improvements to the end customer. Subscription-based remotely hosted software packages make it much easier for software companies to improve their offered product line over a period of time. In addition, customers do not need to worry about hosting the software or keeping it up to date.

Automatic Bill Payment

Automatic bill payments are recurrent money transfers authorized by a consumer to pay specific vendors regularly. Users frequently plan payments to pay various sorts of bills on a month-by-month basis, such as mortgages, credit card bills, installment loans, cell phone bills, energy and water expenses, streaming subscriptions, and so on.

They are also used in B2B transactions for recurring payments for a specific service. For example, a consumer may set up an automatic bill payment at the beginning of every month to pay their automobile loan payments.

How Does Automatic Bill Payment Work?

A consumer can set up automated bill payments in a variety of ways, including through their bank/financial institution, a vendor's website, or cloud-based accounting software, to name a few. Regular payments can be made using a credit card, debit card, or checking/savings account.

Once scheduled, the payment is made directly to the vendor by the customer's banking institution via an e-payment system.

Often, the vendor is granted permission to charge the customer's bank account for the amount outstanding for the designated month. The customer can stop or postpone the automatic payment at any time.

Benefits of Automatic Bill Payment

An automatic payment plan presents many benefits for both a customer and a business. Some of them are listed below:

For Businesses

- **Reduces Business Expenses:** By relocating payment operations online, businesses can save significantly on office supplies such as envelopes, stationery, postage, and so on.

- **Saves Time:** The time spent manually generating bills, contacting clients, processing payments, and investigating late payments can be invested in vital business tasks. Billing operations can be handled by a computer and banking software.

- **Improved Customer Service:** Customers can settle their recurring liabilities and enjoy an improved user experience by using automatic bill payments. In addition, a late fee is rarely applied, which enhances the customer-service provider relationship.

- **Reliable Cash Flow:** Knowing the exact date and amount that will be credited to the company's account allows it to plan and manage its spending more efficiently.

- **Improves Payment Security:** From a security standpoint, verified and encrypted payments by credit card or bank account are preferable to cash or a check mailed in an envelope.

For Customers

- **Improved Credit Rating:** Aside from convenience, time, and money savings, automatic billing can help customers enhance their credit score by making frequent, timely payments to vendors and avoiding late fees and penalties. In addition, customers may be able to better manage their finances if they know the exact date and amount of the weekly or monthly expenses.

How May a Cancellation Be Converted Into a Subscription Reactivation?

Many brands are experiencing fast growth in their subscription businesses. Similarly, businesses have to deal with the problem of canceled subscriptions among their client base and constantly need to minimize it as much as possible. The first stage is determining why a client has canceled subscriptions, but the final goal should be to convert those cancelations into subscriber reactivations.

Subscription Reactivation

A proactive approach to reactivating canceled subscriptions is the first defense against needless churn. Finding ways to interact with customers to learn why they are canceling is a great way to empathize with them while also learning how to improve existing offerings. A canceled subscription can often be reinstated if done correctly.

Starting with a milder approach, such as email or client portal updates, is the first stage in telling clients about new or more tailored offerings. However, those methods may not offer you or your clients the information they need in a timely or actionable manner. To avoid this, service providers can go above and beyond for their customers by executing personalized phone calls to help them stand out as more customer-focused.

How to Avoid Canceled Subscriptions?

Knowing why a client wants to cancel a subscription is extremely valuable information. Furthermore, it lets the company know its clients and how the products fit them. With this vital data, the company is able to not only change its offerings to better meet the demands of its customers but also analyze market shifts.

For example, if customers find the service too pricey, the firm can begin by offering them a discount. This demonstrates concern for the customer's needs and that you are willing to lower your prices to reclaim their business. The risk here is that these particular clients are likely to leave after the discount offer expires and the rate is readjusted.

Another method is to provide different price points. Perhaps the customer's needs have changed, and they no longer require the same quantity of product or service for which they signed up initially. By providing subscribers with additional options, you may be able to re-convert the consumer to a subscription.

Finally, suppose the customer chooses to terminate the service entirely because their use has decreased or they have ceased using it. In that case, open-ended questions on the reasons for the discontinuation can be asked.

Depending on the answers to these questions, you may discover that the only option is to cancel the service entirely; however, providing a stellar customer experience during that process and ensuring customer needs are understood may open them up to reactivation or recommend someone to a new subscription with the company.

Furthermore, this allows organizations to re-evaluate their products and explore gaps in their business models to see whether new offerings may make sense.

Credit Monitoring Services

In the financial world, there are several companies that have services that can afford a subscription-driven model. Of these are several companies that monitor a client's bank accounts for any unauthorized and fraudulent transactions. These companies are called credit monitoring services.

A credit monitoring service monitors borrower behavior to alert consumers to suspected fraud and changes in their creditworthiness.

Fraudsters employ social engineering strategies to gather individuals' personal information to commit identity theft. Phishing, catfishing, tailgating, and baiting are examples of these approaches.

Credit monitoring services can protect against identity theft, which occurs when an individual's information is stolen and used for malicious purposes without the person's permission. For example, when credit card information is stolen and used, a credit monitoring service should recognize the various purchasing patterns and notify the credit card account holder. Experian and Equifax use this model to excel in their field.

What Is Credit Monitoring?

Although credit monitoring services are primarily used to protect consumers from identity theft, they also track a consumer's credit report and credit scores. Identity theft-related criminal behavior can range from making unlawful purchases at retail or online stores using stolen credit card information to filing false Social Security or Medicare claims. Because thieves exploit this information without the victim's knowledge, such criminal conduct can be difficult to identify until long after it has occurred, at which point an individual's credit may be completely destroyed.

The finest credit monitoring services alert clients to changes in their credit activity, such as opening a new account or purchasing a significant item, such as a car. Some credit monitoring services additionally provide more extensive credit score tracking and keeping customers informed about their credit status.

Payment Options

As a courtesy for being a customer, the credit card or bank provides the client with credit monitoring services. Other service providers may provide a basic free service in exchange for a subscription upgrade. Free services may be sufficient for a few account types and credit cards, and if clients don't have significant assets at danger.

A credit monitoring service generally costs between $8.99 and $34.95 a month, depending on the customer's needs and whether they need it on an individual or family basis.

Conclusion

Newspaper and book publishers pioneered subscription business models in the 1600s. However, with the rise of information technology and software as a service (SaaS) product, many businesses are now shifting from a business revenue model in which revenue is generated from a one-time purchase by a customer to a subscription model in which revenue is generated on a recurring basis in exchange for consistent access to the delivery of a good or service.

Subscriptions are now usually automatically renewed and enabled using a pre-authorized credit card or bank account. The advantage of subscription business models is that they generate recurring revenue, which aids in developing strong client connections and provides a business with a decent foundation to grow and forecast future revenues of their ongoing business.

Step 2: A Financing Strategy

Chapter 8: Importance of a Financing Strategy

Many confuse a financial plan to be the same as a company's financial statements. Your financial statements, i.e., Income Statement and Balance Sheet, represent your entity's current financial situation in the case of Balance Sheet or, for a particular time period, let's say, one year if it's your business's Income Statement. However, a financial plan is a vastly different concept. Instead of assessing what has already happened, a financial plan paints a picture of what 'could' happen. It is the difference in time that makes it a wholly unique concept to follow.

What Is a Financial Plan?

A financial plan details the possible financial projections and judgments based on those predictions. Hence, in addition to telling you your current financial status, a financial plan forecasts and makes projections for the coming time. It forecasts your future income and possible outlays to help you in making sound decisions. The projected data acts as an early warning system, helping you to prepare for probable dips in cash flow, ascertain financial needs that might be required, and mitigate the effects of financial uncertainty in business operations.

A financial plan appears as a useful tool in monitoring your finances, allowing you to keep track of your progress and dodge trouble before it has a chance to affect your business.

When pitching to your investors, your financial plan would seek a clear direction for your business, giving your audience a positive impression that you are well-informed on your entrepreneurial agenda. Investors are more likely to fund your operations when they are equipped with certain reassurances that their money will be safe. More than your words, they are likely to believe in numbers, and when your financial plan sets out a positive numerical projection for the future, they will find your entity a more worthy investment.

Cash Flow Statement

The Cash Flow statement is just as important as a profit and loss statement. It is necessary to understand the concept behind a cash flow statement before understanding a financial plan. As we all know, cash is the blood that pumps across the business and keeps it alive. Without maintaining liquidity, it would be impossible for a business to survive. How would you be able to pay for your expenses and current liabilities if you don't have cash? Very low liquidity threatens the entity's ability to continue, and the business will cease to remain operational if this persists over a long period of time.

A cash flow statement explains how much money is flowing into your business and how much money is flowing out. The balances of both inflows and outflows are compared to arrive at a figure termed 'net cash flow.' The net cash flow figure can either be negative or positive depending on the amount of inflows and outflows. In the end, the closing balance is compared with the opening balance to reconcile the net cash flow with the given inflows and outflows. A cash flow statement could be prepared for a month, a year, or several years, depending on the purpose.

You probably may have a hard time running your business if you don't have a clear understanding of how the money is flowing into your business and how it's going out. As cash is the blood of a business, a healthy business can only be assessed through its cash flow statements.

A cash flow statement is a useful piece of information for investors and borrowers. Your investors need to know your net cash flow and evaluate whether the business would be paying them back an adequate return. Your borrowers, characterized by routine lenders such as financial institutions, need to know whether you have enough liquidity to keep up with the interest payments and installments. Without your cash flow statement, it would be hard to predict whether you would be able to secure funds or investments for your business or not.

This statement also provides a comparative analysis of how you can differentiate it from the actual profit and loss statement. The net profit in the profit and loss statement is very different from the net cash flow figure in the cash flow statement, as it reports on the actual cash position of your business.

It is still possible to be profitable but not have enough cash to pay for your expenses and keep it running. This is because the profit and loss statements are prepared on an 'accruals basis.' An accruals concept implies that a business records income when it is earned and records the expenditure when it is incurred. In this case, if you are earning advance income or accruing your debt to the next financial period, it would still be recorded as an income and expenditure. It doesn't matter whether you have received or spent cash—you would still be liable to record an income or expenditure.

How Important Is a Financial Plan for a Business?

As a business owner, everyone wants to establish realistic expectations for their business. They want to make realistic targets backing up their entity's possible successes, which can be measured. If you have already translated your current financial projections, you are less likely to be surprised by the outcome of your current financial state. In addition, your business would be more than prepared to manage a financial crisis and experience sustained growth.

A financial plan also carries a certain appeal to your audience, particularly investors who are more interested in your forecasted income than any other business. The financial plan document shows them that your organization is less of a risk and that you have a firm plan in place to scale your business.

A financial plan also helps in establishing long-term and short-term financial goals. It can be considered one of the profound steps in developing a strategy for your business.

Components of a Financial Plan

A financial plan varies according to the type of business and what exactly should be included in its financial plan. For example, a legal consultancy would have a very different financial plan from an investment management firm. The most suitable financial plan covers the next three years, but it still depends on how long you intend to carry out your business - it is not a general rule of thumb.

Nevertheless, there are some essential components that need to be included in all types of financial planning regardless of the type of business. They are as follows:

- **Sales Projection:** This could be either in a tabular format or explained qualitatively. The figures are the projections for the near future and might as well contain the cost of sales too. You may be able to forecast according to different cost centers, products, and other important aspects to paint a more comprehensive picture.

- **Expenses and budgets:** Business costs are divided into several categories. The broadest classification involves the total cost as being the sum of fixed costs and variable costs. The variable costs are the costs that are directly related to the level of production, i.e., they increase with the production of each additional unit. In contrast, fixed costs are costs that remain the same regardless of the level of production. Whether the business is producing any units or not, the company still must pay for them.

Fixed costs have been a true concern for businesses as they are an important consideration for the business. For instance, the lower the fixed costs, the lower the risk, since a manufacturing business starts earning a profit after it has covered its fixed costs. Fixed costs also play an important role in marginal costing and absorption costing methods - two of the most important tools in cost management and decision-making.

- **Income Statement:** Also known as "Statement of Comprehensive Income" or "Statement of Profit and Loss," an Income Statement specifies the profit earned within a given time period. It documents the list of incomes and expenditures and highlights how the company's net profit is calculated and/or appropriated. As an alternative, you can include a cash flow statement in the financial plan that ultimately achieves the same purpose.

As the income statement would be projecting money inflows and outflows in the form of income and expenditure, the cash flow statement would detail the same thing. Through both ways, you can project the expected income for the next three years in your financial plan.

- **Assets and Liabilities:** The best statement that highlights your assets and liabilities is the Balance Sheet, i.e., Statement of Financial Position. However, in the case of a financial plan, the statement of assets and liabilities would mostly include preliminary expenses and startup costs for infant businesses or resources required for the next expansion strategy.

- **Breakeven Analysis:** This is a very important subject discussed in the domains of cost management, decision-making, and entrepreneurship. A break-even analysis compares the variable costs with fixed costs to determine the level of output where the business can achieve its break-even point. A break-even point is the level of output at which the total sales of the company equals its total expenditure.

Any level of output beyond the break-even point makes a profit for the business. In contrast, an output level below the break-even point would incur a loss. A financial plan of a business, therefore, must detail the break-even analysis of the company so that investors and team members can see how much the targeted output level for your business would be for it to achieve profits.

Your business plan should be able to explain how you intend to achieve the break-even point in the upcoming three years or any specific period that you have mentioned.

Recruitment and Structure of Your Team

Although this element might not be that essential to your business, it does make sense to include this component in your financial plan. The number of employees you intend to hire and the amount of time needed all would constitute a budget. You should be able to ask yourself, who will you need to fulfill your business targets? When should you acquire them? Everything needs to be budgeted if you expect to hire and maintain an additional workforce.

Benefits of Financial Planning

Although it seems rather beneficial to have your business backed up by a financial plan, building it is not easy. A financial plan is prepared through exhausting efforts by the relevant experts who utilize data analytics to draft reliable results. A fair amount of imagination is also involved, driven by real-time data processing. Someone with prior experience in financial planning might tell you that it is very possible that you might hit a few roadblocks along the way.

The prime function of any financial plan is that it keeps teams and employees focused and on track when the entity is expanding. When a business is struck by new challenges or with the forthcoming of an unprecedented crisis, a financial plan would be material enough to walk you out of these types of detriments.

Elizabeth Wasserman, a wealth management client associate for the private executive services team, writes:

"A business plan is all conceptual until you start filling in the numbers and terms. The sections about your marketing plan and strategy are interesting to read, but they don't mean a thing if you can't justify your business with good figures on the bottom line.

The financial section of a business plan is one of the most essential components of the plan, as you will need it if you have any hope of winning over investors or obtaining a bank loan. Even if you don't need financing, you should compile a financial forecast in order to simply be successful in steering your business.[5]"

If you have waited this long to find out what you may gain from business planning, the list could be endless. As more and more financial strategies are developed and/or enhanced consequently, it's possible that you might even lose count of them. However, here are some broad advantages you can identify and experience with a financial plan:

- **Unambiguous and Defined Goals:** Goals and objectives set the premise of any financial plan. To draft a successful plan, you should know what you are hoping to achieve through it.

Ask yourself, what does your business aim to achieve for the following quarter, year, or the next three years?

At the initial stages, a business strives to achieve the 'product/market fit.' For startups, most of them usually take several years until they can achieve the product/market fit. The product/market fit is when businesses try to establish that consumers need their

---

[5] Elizabeth Wasserman, How to Write a Financial Section of a Business Plan, Swinburne University of Technology.
https://www.studocu.com/en-au/document/swinburne-university-of-technology/advanced-innovative-business-practice/howto-write-the-financial-sectionof-business-plan-1/15548301

product and that their business is the provider of the said need.

This is gradually translated into one of your company's primary objectives. Hence, when establishing your ideal product/market fit, you won't be setting lofty sales targets or huge marketing KPIs. There's no point in investing in sales and marketing if you're unsure whether your product will catch any sales.

This brings us back to the benefits obtained through financial planning – a financial plan paves a roadmap for companies to establish identifiable and clear objectives so that the money is invested accordingly and in relevant areas.

- **Cash Flow Management:** One of the most important things offered through financial planning is 'clarity.' If you have clear expectations set in terms of liquidity for your business, your cash flow should accurately reflect the figure. Therefore, a financial plan provides reliable and achievable cash flow forecasts.

At the beginning of your entrepreneurial journey, it is obvious that you would be spending more than you're earning. But what would account for an acceptable level of expense? And how do you intend to stay on track with those expenditures? By making a financial plan, you can anticipate and tackle challenges associated with your cash flow. It would help in many ways in managing your money effectively.

Drafting a successful plan would mean measuring your cash flow with due diligence and professional competence. You may need good financial experts to draft it for you - they should be able to keep track of your entity's money flow accurately and efficiently.

- **Budgeting:** Budgeting is the process of allocating expenditures to different cost centers. It is a strategy that is closely related to cash flow forecasting and cost reductions.

Budgeting is an essential component of financial planning that helps business owners figure out how exactly they are going to spend their money after determining the amount of money they can spend. Every established company has its budget placed for the quarter or a year.

After an overall budget is determined, it is broken down further and allocated to different cost centers, i.e., departments or teams. The significance of the amount that is allocated to each of these cost centers reflects their importance.

This strategy informs business owners of their limits; every business faces a constraint on resources from which they tend to scale up themselves. In that way, they get an idea of the number of resources available to them and can accordingly plan out product development and marketing campaigns.

Allocating a budget to teams and departments is a very useful process as it is relatively easier to keep track of money by appropriating it to different cost centers rather than monitoring expenditure on an entity-wide scale. Breaking down the budget is a relatively straightforward approach as it helps you monitor the sources and items of your business's expenses.

- **Saving Money Ahead of Time:** Financial planning helps business owners to obtain necessary cost reductions for their businesses. It would be comparatively easier for you to control your expenditure if you have been in business for a considerable period. You would have the opportunity to evaluate the expenses that are already incurred by your business and assess how fast your business is expanding.

Cost reductions are more compatible with established businesses as they have been operating for a while and have access to past data. When you set your budget for the next year, you will use your past data to identify expenditures where the cost seems to be too inflated. You will identify expenses that are unnecessary for your business to function and carry no relevance to any profit your business makes – expenses should be aligned with the revenue they generate. After determining unnecessary costs, you will have insights to make changes for the next year's budget. For your entity's unnecessary expenses, you might elect to eliminate them or reduce them to a satisfactory level such that their effect is not pervasive to the profits.

Controlling your expenditure and saving money are all part of the 'spend control' strategy. It is a conscious effort to keep your expenses congruent with your expectations. You may never know when an opportunity may befall you where you will have the chance to make significant cost savings. Therefore, it is recommended to perform a quarterly or annual budget review, after which you can unearth areas where you can save money and where you can devote the appropriate number of resources.

- **Mitigating Risk:** Risk management is a key aspect of financial planning, and it aims to counter the risks of uncertainties disrupting your business's revenue streams. Financial planning renders a business bold enough to make a profitable decision by going beyond those risks.

A finance department in a company helps business owners avoid and navigate risks. Ranging from financial fraud to economic crisis, risks are harder to predict and avoid. There are plenty of risks that we can see coming, but nevertheless, they are equally challenging.

Your business's financial plan can detail several strategies for managing risks effectively. It allows for certain insurance expenses that may cover your entity in unprecedented circumstances. Whether your business is suffering through risky inefficiencies or incurring unexpected expenses, a financial plan ensures that it has covered every corner.

In trying times, a financial plan helps determine several forecasts that show different outcomes for businesses. It could point out ways in which revenue is easy to come by, however, at the expense of uncontrollable costs, or vice versa.

A financial plan is all about having a contingency plan in place. For business owners, it helps them easily modify their business roadmap if they cannot meet their growth targets. Risk management assists you in the expansion process so that you don't go overboard. It is true that you may find plenty of risk factors inside your business, but risk management is there to guide you in coming up with the best response to the situation.

- **Managing Crisis**: When an entity is struck by a severe crisis, the first thing it does is revise and restructure its plans and methodologies, which, of course, bears the most important prerequisite for your organization – you should always have a business plan in place. If your business is not backed by a comprehensive business plan, you won't have many options to handle a crisis other than to improvise.

After the 2020 financial crisis, i.e., one year after the COVID-19 pandemic, the most obvious advice business owners obtained from financial experts was to revise and forecast their figures constantly. Nobody had an idea when the crisis would end and to what extent it would affect their business. Hence, one of the most sudden shifts in trends you would observe in any business today is their practice of regularly creating financial plans – they can be either on a monthly or quarterly basis.

Only those businesses that have created the most comprehensive financial plans, based on knowledge and insights from various industry experts, would have a much easier time in crisis management. If you have a financial plan in place, you do not have to worry about starting all over again whenever your business is faced with a detrimental situation. If your business has a good crisis management methodology in place, you might have already identified the key risk factors to pull in the response.

- **Fundraising Made Easier:** Suppose you are a startup with a sustainable business operation in place, and your business needs a small liquidity injection. You may also be talking about securing a significant series-level investment, for which you need to raise a huge capital investment. Hence, in a bid to raise funds for your agenda, you would present yourself in front of prospective investors. The first thing they would ask from you would be to see your business plan. Your investors will have an interest in how you intend to grow your business, the risks involved in your growth strategies, and how you intend to keep their investment safe.

A financial plan aimed at drawing investors to your side is critical. They are more likely to trust you when your business plan is supported by comprehensive data and analytics. In fact, it doesn't matter whether you are seeking funds or not – a business plan will continue to remain an important tool in your inventory.

- **A Roadmap for Growth:** A financial plan evaluates the current situation of the business and anticipates where your business aims to be in the future. This is also where your business plan would come in handy. A business plan determines the markets in which your business would be able to sell, the size of the workforce you should carry, and the products and services you aim to sell.

Within the business plan, there would be a financial section that would supplement the data to your business goals. For example, if an entity is creating new vacancies for its expansion plan, the financial plan would detail the insights of the recruiters and a specific budget that can help it afford new hires.

All it takes is to give sufficient time and thought to decide how large you want your company to be. You need to decide on your expenses and the projected revenue that you can anticipate flowing into your entity. If you're running an infant business and need a way to help grow financially, you should bear in mind that you might be burning cash a lot faster than you think. However, despite spending piles of money and not being able to reach your growth targets, this may require you to reassess your position. In conclusion, you need to set objectives first and then revise them in response to any developing circumstances.

- **Transparency:** A financial plan details the budgeted expenditure that a company plans for the upcoming period. However, in addition to budgeting, risk management, and cost control, a financial plan has more benefits than we can imagine.

When you read out your plan to your staff, it displays that you are open and honest with your staff about your entity's future. Some startups even go as far as disclosing their salaries to the general public to maintain their audience's trust.

Today's employees want to see their organization managed by competent professionals and know that the entity is on the correct path to success. When you share your financial plan with your team, they will create a dialogue and give their own insights. In this way, a business plan that might be lacking in details would turn out to be a successful one.

Conclusion

Financial planning is one of the key practices observed by affluent entrepreneurs. They form the premise of a very successful business venture as they give a particular direction and aim to a business. A financial plan gives clarity and confidence to business owners and motivates the rest of the workforce by providing them with a target they could work toward. However, a business still needs to carefully draft a financial plan and make sure that it covers all the essential elements so that there are no risks of making the wrong decisions.

Chapter 9: Cash Flow Management

Once your values are clear and business elements are identified, it becomes important for a business – no matter how small or established – to create financial strategies. These are often documents, in terms of plans, that allow you to keep track of your goals and fulfill your vision with expected timelines or milestones. After all, as conventional wisdom puts it, any plan is better than no plan.

Perhaps the most important aspect in a business is to ensure that the business processes continue to run without any derailing interruptions and there are contingencies in place for any untoward incidents or problems. This can be made possible through a managed cash flow, which can be understood as the continuation of the blood flow in the life of a system.

Importance of Cash Flow

Having an effective cash flow system can reflect a healthy business and increase the chances of a business surviving any challenge too. According to a study by the US Bank, a lack of cash is a reason that over eighty percent of businesses fail in their initial seven or startup years.[6] While businesses should concentrate on growing revenue streams, it is equally important to keep a check on your cash flow.

The cash flow system is not only about tracking the inflows against outflows but also about conducting its analysis. The ability to maintain a positive cash flow and to strategize its management is a crucial element of a financially stable business.

The financial health of a business is about identifying trends, preparing for future contingencies, and tackling any issues that may arise as a result of cash flow problems. The best way to prepare for any untoward issues is to analyze how much money is available to the business. This can help identify how much money might be required to maintain both current and future business operations and manage debts accordingly.

The chances of a business failing go up to ninety percent up until its twentieth year.[7] This means that only half of the startups and a tenth of businesses can survive the competition and maintain cashflows. Obtaining loans also becomes difficult with negative

---

[6] Michael Flint, Cash Flow: The Reason 82% Of Small Businesses Fail, Preferred CFO. June 08, 2020. https://preferredcfo.com/cash-flow-reason-small-businesses-fail/

[7] Jeff Desjardins, Here's Why Small Businesses Fail, Business Insider. August 3, 2017. https://www.businessinsider.com/why-small-businesses-fail-infographic-2017-8

cashflows, and a significant chunk of assets or property might need to be deposited to secure a loan in this situation.

Effectively managing cash flows can set a positive trajectory for your business and help you ascertain whether you will be able to expand or not. At the same time, a financial strategy is to not overstress a positive cash flow because it can also hint toward a lack of diversity, investment, and risk by the business. Similarly, a negative cash flow can also indicate unpaid debtors and allow enough time to strategize financial distress and prioritize expenses.

Cash flows allow creditors to evaluate your business's performance or potential investors to gauge the stability of your business. The most useful benefit of maintaining a cash flow is that it allows businesses to align profits with investments continually and leads to stability. A healthy cash flow will lead to increased income and profit and an open window for investors to invest their money in your business.

If you want to ensure that your cash flow improves and you avoid the consequences of a negative cash flow, then follow these tips:

Quick Tips for Managing Cash Flow
- Perform regular cash analysis.

- Adopt regular cash flow reporting.
- Maintain invoice management.
- Process invoices quickly to speed up cash flow.
- Confront cash flow problems early on.
- Have a clear debt strategy, process, and plan.

Business leaders often face unknowns, and they must plan for any unforeseen or unfortunate situation. External factors, such as prices of commodities, inflation, policies, etc., can also have untoward effects on business.

For instance, a bank or guarantor may default due to mismanagement and lead to a stress on your assets or credit stream. Similarly, supply chain issues or the bankruptcy of a debtor can lead to a change in your timelines or business goals. The important question to remain will be: what is your plan for the situation?

Planning

"Do not get yourself overly concerned about what your income statement is showing, or even your tax return in some cases," says small business expert and author Gene Marks. "Be more concerned [about] what your cash flow is."[8]

---

[8] Speaker, Author and Columnist, Gene Marks, Gene Marks website. https://genemarks.com/

The added insights and forecasting for both planned and unplanned changes also need to be incorporated into cashflows. This can be made possible and taken further through the creation of a business plan. It allows businesses to outline any major targets and hurdles and help guide them as to how they may be approached.

It has also been noted that the presence of a structured business plan can improve the chances of securing a form of financing and increase the rate of growth against competition by up to thirty percent![9]

Consider the following scenario: Imagine profit as the theory of your business success and cash flow as the reality. Profit alone cannot pay bills; however, cash that's available to you can do so.

In a personal life scenario, what would happen if you pay your mortgage with a fifteen-day delay because your pay is received late? You would have to pay a surcharge or fine that you probably would not have accounted for. Whether you have enough money or not, you will have a cash flow issue in such a case,

---

[9] What is a Business Plan and Why is it Important?
https://blog.nationwide.com/business/business-starting/importance-of-a-business-plan/#:~:text=Whether%20you%E2%80%99re%20starting%20a%20small%20business%20or%20exploring,marketing%20and%20finance%20to%20operations%20and%20product%2Fservice%20details.

and this is why planning becomes essential – even more so for a business.

"It is the lifeblood of your business," says Denise O'Berry, author of Small Business Cash Flow: Strategies for Making Your Business a Financial Success.[10] "You've got to have money "coming in before you can put money out. That's what cash flow is all about: The in and out of money in your business."

The Business Plan as a Strategy

"If you fail to plan, you are planning to fail."

- Benjamin Franklin

A business plan is a fifteen-to-twenty-page document. It describes how a business aims to accomplish goals and includes information about products, marketing strategies, and finances. You should create a business plan, ideally before the launch of a new business, and it should be continuously updated over time as your business model matures and revenue starts to grow. Business plans metaphorically function as a compass since

---

[10] Small Biz Herald, The Key to Managing Profit and Cash Flow for Your Small Business, The Hartford website. August 10, 2016. https://sba.thehartford.com/finance/managing-profit-cash-flow/

they provide a way to maneuver your business to success and help you avoid going off track.

A business plan helps identify a business's unique selling proposition (USP) and how it can differentiate from the competition in your industry. It also helps one assess the opportunities and threats within the market and how one can leverage or mitigate them accordingly. By conducting a thorough market analysis, one can gain a deep understanding of the target segment and its expectations as well as requirements.

Purchasing patterns and feedback can also be studied and incorporated. This will enable you to tailor your products or services to meet their demands and increase customer satisfaction. This is why owners who have a business plan grow their businesses thirty percent faster than those who don't, and three-fourths of the high-growth companies have business plans and secure financing two and a half times more than businesses without plans.[11]

Instead of putting yourself in a situation where you may have to stop and ask for guidance or even go back and start over, small business owners often use business plans to help them stay on track. That's

---

[11] Entrepreneurship, The Importance of a Business Plan, Waveapps.com https://www.waveapps.com/blog/importance-of-a-business-plan

because they help them see the big picture, plan, make important decisions, and increase the overall likelihood of success.

Why Is a Business Plan Important?

A well-structured business plan is an important tool. In fact, it is almost an asset because it provides entrepreneurs and their employees with the ability to set their goals and measure them against their progress as the business grows. Business planning should be the first thing done when starting a new business. Business plans are also important for attracting investors so they can assess whether your business is on the right path and worth investing in or not.

Business plans typically include detailed information that can help improve your business's chances of success, such as market and competition analyses. An analysis of the market involves collective information about the key players, major factors, and important conditions that affect your industry. A competitive analysis involves an evaluation of the strengths and weaknesses of your competitors.

Ways a Business Plan Helps Improve Operations and Credit Line

A business plan is a vital tool for any entrepreneur who wants to succeed in a competitive market. It helps you to define your goals, strategies, and actions for your business. A business plan also helps you to communicate your vision and value proposition to potential investors, customers, and partners.

Due to the comprehensive and objective nature of business plans, they help prepare and strategize for various things, such as the following:

- **Clears Direction:** A business plan helps you to articulate your mission, vision, and values for your business. It also helps you to identify your target market, customer needs, and competitive advantage. By having a clear direction for your business, you can focus on the most important activities and avoid distractions.

- **Helps Set Realistic Objectives:** A business plan helps you set specific, measurable, achievable, relevant, and time-bound (SMART) objectives for your business. These objectives help track progress and evaluate performance. They also aid in aligning your actions against your desired outcomes.

- **Prepares for Risks :** A business plan prepares a business in identifying and assessing the potential risks that may affect your business. These risks may include market changes, customer preferences, competitor actions, legal issues, financial challenges, and operational problems. By anticipating and mitigating these risks, you can reduce their impact on your business.

- **Secures Funding and Credit Options:** A business plan assists in attracting and convincing potential investors and lenders that your business is worth investing in. It shows them how much money you need, how you will use it, and how you will repay it. It also shows them how profitable and sustainable your business is.

- **Markets Effectively:** A business plan aids in the development of a marketing strategy that is suited to the target market and customer segments. It allows you to define your unique selling proposition (USP), brand identity, and values. It also leads you to identify the best marketing channels, methods, and tools that would be used to reach and retain customers.

- **Optimizes Operations:** A business plan allows the smooth functioning of business operations, from designing to implementing logistics to structuring an operations plan that ensures the smooth running of the production process. It helps one to select the best suppliers, equipment, technology, and staff for the business. It also helps you to optimize the quality, efficiency, and cost-effectiveness of your operations.

- **Manages Cash Flow:** A business plan helps you to prepare a cash flow projection that shows how much money is expected to flow in and out of your business over a period. It allows you to forecast the sales revenue, expenses, and profits for each month or quarter of each year. It also helps you to identify potential cash flow gaps or surpluses that may influence your liquidity.

- **Leads to Strategic Growth:** A business plan eventually helps outline an overall path to long-term growth for your business. In addition, it helps identify new opportunities for expansion and innovation. Furthermore, it allows you to evaluate the feasibility, viability, and desirability of every opportunity. It also helps you to allocate resources, set priorities, and implement action plans for each growth initiative.

- **Depicts the Landscape Clearly:** While you might have a grip on the inner workings of your business, it's essential to realize the exact position of the business and the market behavior in general. Writing a business plan can go a long way in helping you gain a better understanding of your competition than before. The introspective and extrospective nature of the plan can identify consumer trends and preferences. An added benefit is that potential disruptions and other insights that aren't always plainly visible can also be prepared for.

- **Reduces Risk:** Entrepreneurship can be risky; however, the risk becomes significantly manageable once it gets placed against a well-articulated business plan. Drawing up revenue and expense projections, devising logistical and operational plans, and understanding the market and competitive landscape can all help reduce the risk factor from an inherently precarious way to making a living. Having a business plan allows you to leave less up to fate, make informed decisions, and clearly envision the future of your business.[12]

A business plan can help you set realistic goals and milestones for your business growth and track your progress against them. It can also help you identify potential pitfalls or challenges that might arise along the way and prepare contingency plans for them. By having a clear financial plan, you can manage your cash flow effectively, avoid overspending or underinvesting, and secure funding from investors or lenders if needed. A business plan can also serve as a communication tool that showcases your vision, mission, values, and strategies to your stakeholders.

Now that the reasoning behind business plans is clear, one can move forward with creating one's own in a confident and clear manner. Remember that a business plan will grow and evolve along with your business, so it is an important part of the entire journey—not just the start of it.

---

[12] Ibid.

A business plan and a cash flow statement are not a formality that can help secure funding, credit, or insight. Instead, the documents are not to be forgotten and prove to be dynamic tools to help frequently update against changes to both your business and the market. By reviewing and revising your business plan periodically, you can ensure that it reflects your current situation and goals, aligns with changing market conditions and customer needs, and guides you toward achieving success.

Credit – Last but Not the Least

One of the common and often final challenges that entrepreneurs face, after strategy and planning, is how to secure funding for their business – its expansion or operations. Most of the new entrepreneurs believe that possessing a great idea, an ambitious plan, and a passion is enough to convince investors to back them. Research tends to suggest otherwise. Investors are interested in how well an entrepreneur has prepared their business strategy, compared to how well they can defend and articulate it.[13]

---

[13] Chen, X.- P., Yao, X., & Kotha, S. (2009). Entrepreneur passion and preparedness in business plan presentations: A persuasion analysis of venture capitalists' funding decisions. Academy of Management Journal, 52(1), 199-214.

This does not mean, however, that entrepreneurs need to always have a fancy business plan ready at all times. In fact, investors and some creditors do not even bother to ask for one, and many do not even bother to read them, as per Palo Alto's COO - Noah Parsons.[14]

Instead, what this means is that entrepreneurs need to conduct prior planning, whether it is on paper or in their head, and it is only required to reflect a sense of situational awareness and commercial viability — the two most important factors in securing credit. So, focus on answering questions about market opportunities, their value propositions, their competitive advantages, and so on.

This means that an overemphasis on cash flow statements and business plans can derail your plans of securing credit or an investor. Writing a detailed business plan document should be encouraged, although it should focus on creating an internal document that outlines and describes strategies and goals. Entrepreneurs should also prepare a pitch that aims to summarize the salient aspects of the enterprise in a clear, cogent, and constructive manner.

---

[14] Noah Parsons, Do You Need a Business Plan? Scientific Research Says Yes, Bplans.com
https://articles.bplans.com/do-you-need-a-business-plan-scientific-research-says-yes/

The benefit of planning will not only help entrepreneurs become prepared for investors but also help them become more likely to start a business, and this can be a difficult step for many. A study conducted at the University of Oregon found that entrepreneurs with a plan are more likely to launch their business than those who do not have one.[15]

Try to Act Rather Than to Think

Considering the aspects explained above, do not let your ideas remain in the form of dreams. The most important aspect to analyze is to plan to turn your idea into reality. You should know your business from inside and out. Once this ability is achieved, then ideally, there should be no credit lines inaccessible to you.

Remember to have at least an internal document, if not a proper business plan to share, that captures your business strategies and goals. Always prepare a pitch, or have one or two prepared in advance, to showcase and present your business in an engaging manner when in a dire strait or immediate need of a credit facility.

---

[15] Ding, E., & Hursey, T. (2010). Evaluation of the effectiveness of business planning using Palo Alto's Business Plan Pro. Department of Economics. University of Oregon.

It turns out that practice and planning really pay off, so it is crucial to follow it, too. A study published has found that entrepreneurs who take time to create a plan for their business idea are one-hundred and fifty-two percent more likely to start their business than those who do not have a plan.[16] Not only this, but also that entrepreneurs with a plan are also one-hundred and twenty-nine percent more likely to grow and expand their business beyond the initial startup phase.

These findings can be confirmed by another study that found that entrepreneurs with a plan are almost three times more likely to start their businesses.[17] Interestingly, these entrepreneurs are also as likely to close a business. While it seems counterintuitive, it makes sense because it signifies the importance of not only planning but also execution (through a plan) and preparation for a situation of credit insecurity.

Entrepreneurs with everything in place, often keep track of their performance on a regular basis. They know when things do not go as planned, such as when sales are not meeting projections and when

---

[16] Hechavarria, D. M., Renko, M., & Matthews, C. H. (2011). The nascent entrepreneurship hub: Goals, entrepreneurial self-efficacy and start-up outcomes. Small Business Economics, 39(3), 685-701. doi: 10.1007/s11187-011-9355-2

[17] iao, J., & Gartner, W. B. (2006). The effects of pre-venture plan timing and perceived environmental uncertainty on the persistence of emerging firms. Small Business Economics, 27(1), 23-40. doi: 10.1007/s11187-006-0020-0

marketing strategies are failing. The best thing to understand is that entrepreneurs should also know when it may certainly be the time to walk away and try a different idea. This can be rewarding because the energy would be invested in an idea that can turn around for the better.

Chapter 10: Planning for Purchases

It can be understood by now that planning is a crucial aspect of management and that running a successful business requires both a robust business plan and a sustainable cash flow. This is why the cornerstone of success in business is how well the finances are managed because it is what provides stabilization to the operations. Stability and foresight are, therefore, required for future growth and planning.

A significant majority of entrepreneurs do not structure their business well or create comprehensive financial and operational strategies.

This is what makes a robust business plan even more important because it also contains guidelines for handling both receivables and payables. The plan also ensures that an entrepreneur and their business managers can continue to focus on day-to-day operations and progress toward the vision.

This is where having a detailed plan comes in handy. It can help you make the most of the working capital you have and aptly utilize the best financing option when you require additional capital to grow. It can also help you get done with the relatively trivial or operational things that matter and require details.

Ascertaining Credit Lines

So, one might wonder what else can a business require a detailed strategy for, given that we have already discussed some of the fundamental aspects of management. The elements that we are about to discuss and hold importance in a business plan are how purchases and payments will be handled. This is one of the steps toward establishing a successful business plan.

Clarifying the structure of how payments, especially large ones, are handled and what treatment they receive entails that everything flows smoothly. This is an increasingly popular and practical step to follow since under eighty percent of startups have little to no extra financial assistance or aid. Also, it would be inappropriate to search for options and inefficient to create a strategy just before a large purchase is necessary or imminent.

The best way to decide where to start or what to prioritize in purchases is to align or assign short and long-term goals in the hope of fulfilling personal or professional financial planning regardless of what you plan to buy, market, or acquire. The purchases must fall in line with your business plan and be paid in a structured manner to not disturb your cash flow.

The key is to prioritize and balance your goals in the hope of attaining long-term financial success. With your business plan ready, you will be ready to launch your business or expand it, and you will need to identify a diverse range of financing options. It may be used in acquiring raw materials or products to create a finished good or service.

Often, small business owners only have internal financing options available to them, such as their life savings, personal loans, and investor funding. Short-term loans and overdrafts can be made available in cases where an entrepreneur possesses an asset to back against the financing – property, an expensive painting, a royal heirloom, treasury certificates, etc. The main reason for external financing to be backed is that either the business has not established enough - to yield a stable and guaranteed return - or it is mismanaged in terms of a negative or unstable cash flow.

This deters the creditors from providing finance or credit guarantees. With external financing options such as a loan or an equity stake, it is often secured through investment against a stake in ownership or a guarantee in the form of an asset as a deposit for the loan.

The problem with external financing is that it's a debt or, in some cases, tied to equity, which has hidden costs that often vary from service charges to penalties. Depending upon the economic conditions, the debt can become brutal, such as a hike in interest rates will lead to expensive installments, and a rise in inflation will lead to a contraction in disposable income.

A hidden manner of financing is through customers and sales. Loyal and large clients can often be reached out to provide an affordable way of financing, such as through advance payments against existing products/services and upselling or through contracts that ensure a seasonal rollover of payments.

Law Insider's website defines 'Purchased Receivables' as all the rights to payment and their proceeds (all of these are called "receivables") that come from the invoices and other agreements that the Seller gives to the Buyer with any Invoice Transmittal that the Buyer chooses to buy and pays an advance for.[18]

Preparing for Large Purchases

It becomes essential to plan out how and what sort of credit procedures would be adopted because an established line will mean operations run smoothly. What an entrepreneur starts early on will impact the business in the long run since these business traditions continue to become practices in a year or after a couple of years.

---

[18] Law Insider, Purchase Receivables Definition, Lawinsider.com https://www.lawinsider.com/dictionary/purchased-receivables

That's why having a successful business and financial plan is strategically important. Without one, you may spend your time managing day-to-day operations without seeing the bigger picture. Your business may begin to stagnate, if not deteriorate, rather than grow.

The question after ascertaining credit lines is to associate them with expected categories of costs. For instance, the purchase of heavy machinery or a plant might be financed through a long-term bank loan, whereas that of a car might be through a one-time payment or lease.

Large purchases, such as that of long-term assets, overhauling, or renovation efforts, are usually conducted to substantially increase revenues in the least amount and consistently over a long period.

The question remains as to how a large purchase will be conducted and what its preparation should be.

When and how should such a purchase be initiated? Will the entire payment be paid in advance or through a loan agreement? Additional staff are also hired and trained when making large purchases, and increases in prices and profits can follow suit.

This is why the purchase of expensive equipment is meant to be planned for months, if possible, gradually implemented and assessed by your experts.

It is important to figure out whether an asset needs to be bought or hired in the business. The accountants can explain in detail and paint a picture of the possible options too. They will be able to easily reflect if a purchase is suited to the cash flow too.

These tips fall under financial strategy in the business plan, which has grown as the ultimate objective. It can also be possible through a business acquisition or a mortgage.

While one may not be able to afford an entire office building, with the right cash flow management and credit-building strategies, you can set the trajectory of your company to take out financing at a low rate for a long period of time.

Determining Payment Method

When you want to buy something expensive, you need to think about how to finance it. There are different ways to pay for the cost, such as cash, a credit card, or a personal loan. The best way depends on how much the item costs.

Paying with cash may not be feasible if you don't have enough money available for a large purchase. A credit card may be a good option for buying big items because you can get rewards and avoid paying interest for a certain period.

For example, the U.S. Bank Visa® Platinum Card offers 0% intro APR for 18 billing cycles (after that, 18.99% - 28.99% variable).[19] You must transfer your balances within 60 days of opening your account.

If you want to enjoy both 0% intro APR and rewards, you can avail a card such as American Express Cash Magnet® Card that gives you an unlimited 1.5% cash back on all eligible purchases, plus an intro 0% for the first fifteen months on purchases from the date of account opening (after that, 18.49% to 29.49% variable APR).[20]

See rates and fees about the most recommended and best credit cards as of March 2023 by CNET.com.[21] Light Stream offers a *6.99% to 23.99% APR (when you sign up for autopay), and terms range from 24 to

---

[19] **Note:** Information about the credit cards, especially American Express Cash Magnet® Card and Capital One Shopping, has been collected independently by CNBC and has not been reviewed or provided by the credit card companies prior to publication.

Payment information can vary time to time, depending on interest rates, bank charges and your credit history. Please do confirm payment information and schedules before finalizing a payment or availing a deal. For additional information about credit card comparisons and decision-making of a purchase, visit the following source:
Alexandria White, 4 Questions to Ask Yourself Before Making a Big Purchase, CNBC. February 10, 2023.
https://www.cnbc.com/select/questions-to-ask-yourself-before-making-a-big-purchase/

[20] Cynthia Paez Bowman, Best Credit Cards for Large Purchases for March 2023, Cnet.com. March 01, 2023.
https://www.cnet.com/personal-finance/credit-cards/best/best-credit-cards-for-large-purchases/

[21] Ibid.

144 months. This can help you finance large purchases at an affordable interest rate.[22]

Another option is a personal loan that gives you a lump sum of cash that you pay back over a set term with interest. Personal loans usually have longer repayment periods and lower interest rates than credit cards - except for 0% APR offers. The current average interest rate for a two-year personal loan is 9.65%, compared to 16.28% for a credit card, as per the Federal Reserve System.

One piece of advice that beats them all is to always be prepared and have a financial strategy that helps you carve your path to success.

Helpful Strategies for Receivables and Payments

Now, let's dive into some of the strategies that small business owners can use to flourish their companies.

---

[22] **Note:** The Light Stream's loan terms, including APR, may differ based on loan purpose, amount, term length, and your credit profile. Excellent credit is required to qualify for lowest rates. Rate is quoted with AutoPay discount. AutoPay discount is only available prior to loan funding. Rates without AutoPay are 0.50% points higher. Subject to credit approval. Conditions and limitations apply. Advertised rates and terms are subject to change without notice.
Payment example: Monthly payments for a $10,000 loan at 7.99% APR with a term of 3 years would result in 36 monthly payments of $313.32.

Prioritize Financial Health from the Beginning

Whether you just started the business or are a startup, it's important to set strategies that help achieve financial success from the start. The foremost is to invest in accounting software and open a business account at a bank so you can separate your personal and business finances.

New businesses may not qualify for some financing options from banks and SBA lenders, so work on building up your credit by opening an account and using business credit cards responsibly.

Set Up a Payment Policy and Direct Debit

Clients running late on their payments can really take a toll and jeopardize your business's cash flow. This is why it's important to establish a policy outlining when invoices are due and what terms and conditions apply to each deal. One strategy that small businesses often forget to adopt is to structure payments by installments and charge a surcharge on non-payments and delays.

The first thing that you should do regarding your recurring payments, such as installments and rent, is to set up a direct debit facility through a bank. This allows an account to have its money deducted as soon as a payment date is due. All you need to do is provide the bank with your payment schedule in writing or seek help when setting up one through a branch or a mobile application.

For your clients' payments, consider charging a late fee to encourage clients to pay on time, or offer a discount instead if you do not want to lose out on their loyalty if they pay early. A surcharge, on top of a fine, should be charged for any payments that are consecutively delayed or rejected. Adopting these policies will keep your cash flow healthy and positive and your liquidity flowing.

On the other hand, the incentivizing payment process is also a relatively trivial aspect but one that is quite helpful and productive. Automating your clients' account payments, such as asking them to set up payment schedules and stand to assist them as much as possible with your accounts receivable processes. Accepting debit and credit cards, as well as bank transfers, lets you get paid digitally, so you don't have to wait for a check to arrive in the mail. On the contrary, accept cheques and cryptocurrency, too, because no payment option should be left out of reach of your customers.

Hire Help to Recover Money and Manage Accounts

Even a small business can benefit from bookkeeping help, especially if you don't have the time to update your accounts regularly.

You can hire a part-time accountant, CPA, or bookkeeper to ensure that your business expenses are appropriately categorized. The clerical and repetitive work, such as sending invoices, following up on late payments, and even filing your taxes, can take much of your precious time. Save time and leave things to professionals whenever you can.

Focus on your business because that is the most important task at hand and what your business requires from you too! The time you save while not having to manage your company's finances is time you can reinvest in running your business. For financial matters, you can also consider hiring a financial advisor who can help you establish your business' financial goals and determine how to best reach them.

Understand Your Financial Statements

Things like cash flow statements, balance sheets, and profit and loss statements might sound complicated. Financial matters and confusion should not be avoided and should always be discussed with professionals. You can have your accountant deal with these matters, but it's important that you, as the business owner, understand your financial statements.

These statements tell the story of your business's financial well-being. Looking at assets and liabilities, cash flow, or projected sales paints a picture of where your business is and where it's headed so that you can make decisions to course-correct when needed

Constantly Monitor Your Credit

Even if your business isn't a new one, it's important to keep an eye on both your personal and business credit. If you haven't yet established credit for your business, spend time learning how to establish business credit since some lenders look at your scores when determining whether to give you financing or not.

Make sure there are no discrepancies, such as payment delays, defaults, or unpaid expenses, in your credit reports. If they are, report them immediately since they can negatively affect your credit. Work to raise your credit scores by paying down debt and making on-time payments each month.

The higher your credit scores, the lower the interest rate you will qualify for should you decide to take out a loan one day.

Consider Your Financing Options

Whether you need an injection of cash right now or not, there may come a day when you do. Maybe you will want to purchase another business in a few years, hire more help, or amp up your marketing spending. Don't wait until then to research your options and find the type of small business loans or lines of credit that are the best fit.

If you run a startup, also investigate venture capital, though bear in mind that any investor will have a piece of your company's equity and may want a hand in the decision-making process.

How to Create a Financial Strategy for Your Small Business

We've covered some tactics you can use to take your business to success. Now, let's build that into a financial strategy.

If you haven't yet created a business plan, now is the time to do so. There are many free templates available online, so use one of them as a starting point. In your small business plan, outline your business goals and how you will achieve them. Leverage those financial statements that you're now an expert at deciphering.

Once you finalize your business plan, don't stick it in a drawer and forget about it. It needs to be a living, breathing document and one that you update as your business pivots.

Successful entrepreneurs know they must see beyond the short-term to develop a business strategy that plans for the long-term financial health of their companies.

Reap the Benefits of Modern Payment Solutions

One of the common options that you may encounter when you shop online is a loan at the point of sale or a POS loan. This is a type of financing that lets you split your purchases into smaller payments over time, either with a one-time installment loan or a payment plan. Some companies that offer POS loans are Klarna and Affirm. These loans usually do not charge interest, but you should always read the terms carefully and know how they affect your credit score.

Conclusion

When you make a large purchase, it is wise to look for any opportunities to reduce the cost. If it cannot really happen in your business because you are new, you can still save up money in your office or home. You can try searching Google for coupons or installing shopping-related browser extensions, such as PayPal Honey or Capital One Shopping, that automatically apply valid discount codes at checkout.

If you do not need to purchase right away, you may want to wait until there is a big sale. Many holidays have special deals, such as Memorial Day sales with discounts on grills and outdoor furniture. Sometimes, retailers also offer friends and family sales that have great savings.

If you use a rewards credit card to pay, you can redeem your rewards for statement credit and lower your bill. For example, if you spend $1,000 on a card that earns 5% cash back, you can get $50 back, which is not bad.

The financial strategy that you adopt should eventually explain how to collect the money, and the business should incorporate what methods and conditions apply to payments. Remember that the goal of having a business plan is to have strategies, vision, and guidelines in place to help efficiently run a business.

Such plans also help management to successfully run the business while you may be away or unavailable. Following the business plan well and creating a robust financial regime will increase the value of the business by finding a balance between liquidity, risk, and profitability.

The prime objective of running a business is to maximize the value of an enterprise and lower costs by striking a balance between liquidity, risk, and profitability. The credit sale bolsters up sales but is attached with the cost of dispensation of credit facilities and collection of accounts receivables.

Lastly, you should also design an appropriate collection policy for the firm after you have completed your business plan. The basic objective is to ensure the earliest possible payment of receivables without any customer losses through ill will. The overall objective of setting up a financial policy for payments and receivables is to minimize the costs and investments in the recovery process.

The receivables and bad debt losses will be greatly reduced with the suggestions put forth in this chapter. If your customers trust you, you should oblige them, and your business will be creditworthy. This will make it less likely for your business to shut down due to financial or management misconduct and issues. If anything, when the set guidelines and policies are clearly identified, outlined, and followed, then success should follow suit.[23]

---

[23] Urmila K., Financial Strategy, Business Management Ideas. n.d. https://www.businessmanagementideas.com/strategic-management/financial-strategy/21040

Chapter 11: Big Picture Considerations

As discussed in the previous chapters of this section, a financial strategy is an underlying foundation that each business needs to guide its workforce and reach eventual success. In the grand scheme of things, the financial strategy will always be all-encompassing and dynamic to incorporate changes in the future. From managing procurement to allocating and utilizing funds, this strategy is what determines how smooth the financial flow will be.

The entire point is to enable an efficient flow of finances that allows the fulfillment of all operational finances of an organization. A financially efficient organization can lead to the maximization of both revenue generation and utilization. This means that finances need to be always well-managed if a business's potential is to be utilized.

Financial Strategy as Part of a Business Plan

Like your business plan, your financial strategy will need to incorporate and focus on financial resources, cost structure, profit projection, accounting standards, etc. It is these things that will allow your business plan to be executed at will and collect accurate data that leads to realistic costs and profit estimations. All of this will allow you to efficiently execute operations as per your needs and context.

In short, a financial strategy pertains to the recognition of how your funds will be sourced, allocated, and utilized. Your business's commercial and management objectives are also aligned with financial stability. This is what can mean the difference in the organization's competitive advantage over the market.

Your business has three main benefits of incorporating a financial strategy:

- Ability to forecast finances.
- Assess key indicators to determine drivers of growth.
- Prepare for the capital requirements.

The reason that business plans present a vision means that financial strategy should also remain future-oriented. This should ideally translate into the fulfillment of short-term goals that smoothly transition toward medium and long-term goals, ensuring financial management along the way. It is the reason why financial management must not focus on the short-term; instead, it is a forward-thinking approach wherein long-term growth is prioritized to secure a sustainable financial future.

These strategies should primarily be understood as principles that your business can adopt to derive maximum gains out of the financial processes. Depending on your company's vision, requirements, and access, the financial strategy can be altered to suit your business's needs. After all, the ultimate objective of your financial strategy is to provide avenues to obtain the most profits and value from business operations.

Other aspects of finance include reporting, projection, analysis, and forecasting. Various financial aspects are also managed through the strategy to aid in decision-making for other activities. Financial strategies ensure that a business's development is in line with the growth in other divisions of the business.

Importance

The main strategic benefit of adopting strategies to guide the financial management of your business is that goals are met. Crucial aspects are identified that can be measured against set criteria for your business interests to be maximized.

The importance of financial management strategies lies in helping you develop a vision for your company's success. It helps you establish a set of control principles under which your company can measure its performance and allow for smooth operations. The reason for this is that each business activity almost always involves assets and liabilities.

Your business plan is what ties income, financing, cash flow, and payment procedures together. This is why it is important to align your business objectives with your financial strategy and set the rules for how you will fund and run commercial activities. Without a decent financial strategy, business strategy can be difficult to work with.

Once you set up your financial strategy, it is quite useful because it can help you evaluate your business's performance and ascertain whether the set goals are realistic or not. The projections can help you prepare for future changes and analyze where your finances are being allocated. Financial strategy is just part of a business plan that prepares and helps you with both expected and unexpected challenges.

Your financial strategy is extremely crucial. If rightly planned and evaluated, it can help you with a lot of different areas of your business, such as the following:

- Highlight any financial risk(s).
- Present financial standing.
- Assess the requirement for additional funds to finance operations.
- Target financial goals.

- Identify additional sources of revenue and credit.
- Indicate the need to explore new avenues to fulfill objectives.
- Establish the required skillset required to maintain objectives.
- Maintain the cash flow and balance expenditure over income.

Ways Financial Strategy Helps

Dividend

A dividend strategy is a way to ascertain the profit-sharing percentage that is to be provided to shareholders after allocations to reserves for future investments are made. This strategy is utilized to allow for maximum gains for shareholders after the necessary capital is allocated to future investments. Due to the low risk involved, it is a strategy utilized to incur the least cost to raise capital and strike a balance between current returns and capital gains.

Capital Structure

Capital is structured in different forms to utilize different aspects, such as retained earnings, equity, preference share capital, and debt capital. These structures are collectively known as the capital structure of a business. The strategy utilizing these structures is used to manage the pros, cons, and risks associated with them.

Capital Budgeting

Also known as investment planning, capital budgeting is a strategy that deals with the process of investing in capital. Following the acquisition of capital, the next step is to invest it, and it is usually in the form of long-term assets. This form of strategic financial management aims to establish, grow, diversify, and enhance a business. The process involves practices such as the sale and replacement of unnecessary or obsolete long-term assets.

Working-capital Planning

Working capital is what deals with everything about the management and procurement of cash in your business. This is used to manage allocations and the future needs of the business. Together, this is your planning strategy for working capital, and it is responsible for your business's cash flow management. This strategy ensures that enough working capital is maintained to fulfill the day-to-day operations of the business.

Other Strategies

To ensure smooth financial management, the adopted strategies need to be aligned with the approach and reviewed periodically. The efficiency of our strategies depends on their realistic and goal-oriented formulation. There are also a few financial elements that need to be considered and tailored along the way.

Financial Analysis

It is crucial to routinely evaluate financial statements and to be on the lookout for important aspects. The ability of a business to engage with financial statements and review them provides an accurate analysis and understanding of the performance. This allows for an appropriate action per data and evaluation of strategy.

This practice can help align strategies with your goals, and these financial decisions are significant because they allow your business's financial position to be visible and provide a general idea of financial performance. It reflects on the set objectives and if they are being met or not.

Together, the statements provide an understanding of the cash flow performance of the business and its usage. A periodic and annual review will help highlight the main elements that drain or bring in revenue. With the help of this strategy, you can make evidence-based decision-making and proactively set future objectives.

Profit and Loss Evaluation

It is not just important to evaluate the statements to ascertain the cash situation. Instead, it is equally significant to analyze your income statements to ascertain profits or losses. A financial strategy cannot lead to effective management if the profits and losses are not ascertained. It is a significant step in strengthening your financial management.

Profit and loss can help indicate what may be significantly good or bad about your business. For instance, if your business has a high cash flow but a low profit or high loss, then it may be indicative of a lack of recent sales or profitable investments. Income statements provide an overview of your business and act as a measurement tool too.

Your business costs, revenue, gross profit, expense, and net profit are visible in the income statement. This can allow for appropriate readjustments to business goals.

General Budgeting

Your business should have executives who can assess and anticipate the costs and revenue. This helps in setting realistic targets and expenses. Your business objectives and profits will also be met accordingly.

This strategic element helps in dividing your team's responsibilities and providing them with their targets. This can be used to allocate budgets, evaluate performance, and redirect attention as per the situation.

A clear and tangible budget is what can accurately track your business's performance over time. Making informed decisions and initiatives is the best outcome of effective budgeting.

Monitoring Receivables

A company gains receivables, or debtors, as it continues to do business over time. These are often clients or institutions that are provided with relief in payment schedules in recognition of their loyalty or value, which results in a credit purchase facility.

The ability to determine credit lines, credit-purchase limits, and the method to recover them is all part of financial planning. How well this strategy is planned will determine the efficiency of your business's financial management.

Tracking Expenses

The ability to track your business's expenses means that you know what financial obligations will be required down the road. This can include visibility over salaries, other ongoing expenses, or credit-related payments. Your company's payroll, along with other regular expenses, is quite important to be tracked.

Employing an automated system, which can be bought or created in-house, can be utilized to conduct payments, or a direct-debit facility can be set to incur such payments. This ensures that important and running expenses are paid on time, and major or new expenses can be frequently reviewed. Having an efficient system will mean that payments are made quickly, with less chance of a fine or repercussions, and incurred expenses appear in real-time in the books.

Summing Up

This chapter provided you with details related to the importance of cash flow, income statements, and financial strategies in the overall management of your business. Anticipation of expenses against those incurred can help reflect the performance of the teams involved and your business objectives. Having a sound financial plan will certainly lead to a controlled environment that allows you to manage a business well.

This means that your business plan can continue to function unhindered, and the teams involved can continue to engage without any hesitation or concerns. Modern companies need to have appropriate and efficient structures to retain the best professionals who can guarantee the success of a business and financial plan. Appropriate goals and objectives can be set and aligned with the help of accurate data.

This leaves less room for error. A business can then continue to take calculated risks to achieve success and compete well in its respective market. If a financial strategy works well and continues over time, then this can lead to an expansion even if the owner may be busy setting up another company or tending to other commitments.

Today's employees want to see their organization managed by competent professionals and know that the entity is on the correct trajectory. When you share your financial plan with your team, they create room for dialogue and provide their insights. This is a useful strategy to improve and evaluate your strategies, which might be lacking in detail but turn out to be successful.

Financial planning forms the core of a business. It is given priority by new and old entrepreneurs alike. It can lead ventures to become successful or help steer a struggling one to head in a positive direction. A financial plan provides clarity and confidence to all the stakeholders in a business.

Providing a team with a tangible target and having up-to-date information means a business can easily recover from an undesirable situation or quickly transition to improvement. A business still needs to carefully draft a financial plan and ensure that it covers all the essential elements so there are no risks of making the wrong decisions and can be effectively created and run.

Chapter 12: Raising Capital

One of the most important decisions for any business is to decide how to raise capital. Capital is the money that is used to start, operate, and grow an enterprise. There are different ways to raise capital. Each one has its own merits and demerits. Some of the most common ways that a business can raise capital are explained in this chapter for the benefit of business owners.

Businesses must plan for their future and anticipate ways of improving profits or growing in an industry. This often leads decision-makers and stakeholders to decide where to spend reserves and how to obtain additional funds to finance long-term expenses. The decisions for this involve instances of buying machinery that may last for ten years or setting up a manufacturing plant that may last for the next forty years.

No matter what the industry is, financing long-term projects involves a lot of research and careful consideration of development costs. In order to source the required funds, which are often humungous, firms can raise capital through four simple categories: early-stage/seed funding from investors, retained profits from previous years, borrowing from banks and bonds, and selling/floating company shares. When planning to finalize a source of capital, a business also needs to consider how repayment would be done and what impacts it would have on the business.

How Raising Capital Works

For businesses that have just started to work on a product or service, whether it is currently functional (in a prototype stage) or restricted to an idea, a certain investment is required to run the firm into a profitable and scalable project of the future. This stage is the most difficult for entrepreneurs because conventional methods of borrowing do not work at this stage.

The ability to pay back, show sales, and history are all the elements that conjoin to ascertain an ability to receive and repay a loan. It will also help set how the return on investment would work. The problem for startups and small businesses is that the primary source of capital is the entrepreneur or business owner himself.

To better understand this, consider if someone decides to start a supermarket. The person will likely cover the startup costs with their personal savings and accounts. Financing is often difficult to be granted in this case, and a collateral such as a house or plot of land will have to be kept as 'a security deposit'.

This is what leads individuals to turn to seed investors and angel investors who are open about their money and its investment. Notable cities around the world have been known to possess a network of well-to-do individuals known as 'angel investors.' These investors inject their money into the new companies from an early stage of development in exchange for owning a stake in the business.

Venture Capital (VC) is a form of financing that allows investors to fund or seed enterprises and startups that showcase the potential to excel in the future. VCs tend to fund early-stage start-ups and innovative ideas in the hopes of scaling their success in the future. VCs take up a fixed percentage of a company's ownership, similar to bonds, but without the need to have a fixed rate of return or an expiration of contract/return on the entire investment.

The reason for the exchange of stake, or a share in the business, is due to the organization's lack of history of attracting significant revenues and earning profits. Without these two things, a business cannot make a credible promise to pay interest. This is why it becomes possible for the business to borrow money. There are two common ways of borrowing capital, which are either through bank loans or bonds.

A bank loan for a firm works in much the same way as a loan for an individual who is buying a car or a house. The firm borrows an amount of money and then promises to repay it, including some rate of interest, over a predetermined period of time. If the firm fails to make its loan payments, the bank (or banks) can often take the firm to court and require it to sell its buildings or equipment to make the loan payments.

If yours is an incorporated business, it would mean that it is owned by shareholders who have limited liability in case of a company's debt and the risk divided as per their shares in the profits and losses. Corporations can be either private or public, and the shares may not necessarily have been publicly traded or owned.

The corporation may raise funds to finance its operations or investments via the selling of stock or issuance of bonds — essentially documents that are 'IOUs' that define a fixed rate of return. The only difference with a bond is that it indicates an expected time of maturity.

Once a stock changes hands, a buyer can become a legal owner in the firm. The stocks represent ownership in the business. Enterprises can have millions of stocks in the case of medium-to-large corporations. Instead, large numbers of shareholders—even those who hold thousands of shares—each have only a small slice of the firm's overall ownership.

Merits and Demerits of Raising Capital

The benefit of raising capital through a share in equity, also known as equity financing, is that there is no loan to repay. This translates to less burden on the firm to repay a principal amount (investment), and there are no monthly interest payments. Also, any credit issues due to a poor or lack of history are also bypassed.

This means that the business, in turn, is free to concentrate on business operations and growth. This will help you learn and gain from the advice and guidance of the investors. This presents an opportunity to form informal partnerships that will grow over time and present more knowledgeable or experienced resources.

Some might be well-connected, allowing your business to potentially benefit from their knowledge and their business network. These investors can also advise on common pitfalls and things to look out for when growing.

While a business is backed up with external funding, internal funding, and resources can be preserved for other purposes, such as cash payment to vendors, which can add up to the company's credit score, or for human resources training, which can improve the efficiency of employees.

External funding gives you the liberty to remain private rather than go public to raise funds. It also requires less investment of both money and time than in public ventures. A company can raise many rounds of funds when they stay private.

Your investors will expect – and deserve – a piece of your profits. However, it could be a worthwhile trade-off if you are benefiting from the value they bring as financial backers and/or their business acumen and experience. The price to pay for equity financing and all its potential advantages is that you need to share control of the company. Sharing ownership and having to work with others could lead to some tension and even conflict if there are differences in vision, management style, and ways of running the business. It can be an issue to consider carefully.

Investors require a return on their investments. They add up their interests to the investment made in a company; this can also prove to be a financial burden for a start-up at times if things don't work out as per the plan. Securing external funding can be very lengthy and complex as well. Searching for the right investors can be a big task. The process includes preparing a business plan, pitching the VCs, preparing financials, and so on. It is also very time-consuming.

They can also pull out their financial support if they do not seek any growth as planned. The funding is very uncertain as there is no guarantee of time a VC may stay in a company. If their money is recovered, they may exit at any time.

Capital Strategies

Capital-raising strategies are methods that businesses use to obtain the funds they need to grow and achieve their goals. There are different types of capital-raising strategies, depending on the stage, size, and industry of the business, as well as the availability and cost of capital. Some of the common capital-raising strategies are:

Self-fund operations. This is when the business owner uses personal savings, assets, or income to fund the business. This is the simplest and cheapest way to raise capital, as it does not involve any interest, fees, or external obligations. However, it also limits the amount of capital available and exposes the business owner to personal risk if the business fails.

The second way is to restructure or finance an existing debt. This is when the business borrows money from a lender, such as a bank, an online platform, or a family member or friend. The business must repay the loan with interest over a period of time. Debt financing can provide a large amount of capital quickly and easily, and it does not dilute the ownership or control of the business. However, it also increases the financial burden and risk of the business, as it has to make regular payments regardless of its profitability or cash flow.

As discussed above, equity financing is a common method, but these days, it can also come through a crowdfunding platform. The business does not have to repay the money or pay interest, but it must share its profits and decision-making power with the investor. Equity financing can provide a large amount of capital and access to valuable expertise and networks from the investor. However, it also reduces the ownership and control of the business owner and may involve complex legal and regulatory requirements.

Crowdfunding is a way of raising small amounts of money from many people, usually through an online platform. Crowdfunding can be used for various purposes, such as launching a new product, supporting a social cause, or testing a market demand. Crowdfunding can be equity-based, where investors receive a share of the business in exchange for their contribution, or reward-based, where investors receive a product or service as a reward.

This is a way of raising large amounts of money from a group of investors who pool their resources and share the risk and reward of the investment.

Syndicated investors can be angel investors, venture capitalists, or private equity firms who have expertise and connections in a specific industry or sector. Syndicated investors can provide mentorship, guidance, and access to networks for the businesses they invest in.

Private equity, via venture firms, can mean investment in a business that is not publicly traded, and often, a majority stake is bought out or issued as a loan. Private equity funds typically invest in mature businesses that have stable cash flows and growth potential, while debt funds typically invest in businesses that need short-term financing or restructuring. Private equity or debt funds can help businesses improve their operations, expand their markets, or acquire other businesses.

Small Business Administration (SBA) financing is a way of raising money from the U.S., which guarantees loans made by banks and other lenders to small businesses that meet certain criteria. SBA financing can be used for various purposes, such as starting, expanding, or acquiring a business, purchasing equipment or inventory, or refinancing debt. SBA financing can offer lower interest rates, longer repayment terms, and lower down payments than conventional loans.

Lines of Credit are revolving loans that allow businesses to borrow up to a certain limit and repay it as needed. Bank lines of credit can be used for short-term working capital needs, such as paying suppliers, covering payroll, or managing cash flow fluctuations. Bank lines of credit also offer flexibility, convenience, and lower interest rates than credit cards or overdrafts.

Summing Up

Finally, family donations, gifts, or even loans can also be obtained to support a business. Often, friends and family are those who support our business ideas and want to help succeed them. Family donations can be used for any purpose related to the business, such as launching, growing, or overcoming challenges. Family donations can offer emotional support, trust, and loyalty, but they can also pose risks of conflict, misunderstanding, or loss of relationship.

Lastly, there are some questions that you can ask yourself or advise someone you know who may be in the process of securing financing for their business. The foremost is to understand whether you want to operate solely on your discretion, without compromising on decision-making or not. The next step is to consider whether a formal mode of financing, such as a loan, would be easily repayable or not.

If you are ready to share profitability and decision-making, then opt for a healthy business relationship.

The methods discussed in this chapter are some of the ways that businesses can utilize to secure financing and structure strategies to achieve their business goals. What is important to note is that every method has its own pros and cons. Just like other business decisions, each financing option should be carefully evaluated against needs and weighed against the risks before finalizing an option. Professional help and a financial consultant's advice will go a long way too.

Step 3: Marketing System

Chapter 13: Introduction

A business plan is a blueprint for taking an idea for a product or service and turning it into a commercially viable reality. Other than having a business and a financial plan, enterprises should also have a marketing plan prepared. It should ideally include the following four key areas: product, pricing, promotion, and place.

The marketing plan helps to identify your clientele and how a business aims to attract them. This is what creates the difference in how customers decide to purchase the offered products and services or not.

One of the easiest ways to develop a marketing plan is to work through each of the parts that make up a marketing plan. Also, significant market research needs to be conducted to identify the important aspects of the target audience and how to market to them. This is a bit more rigorous compared to when we create the other sections of the business plan.

Along with the information about the market segment and target audience, there is also a need to identify competitors and conduct an analysis of their presence. Your business can only gain the attention of consumers after you have identified the uniqueness of your product or service and targeted them.

This will allow you to showcase your product differently and show the consumer what they might receive when they avail of what you offer. This is why it is often crucial to think about things openly and rigorously, though, when planning to create a marketing plan.

Creating a Marketing Plan

Conventional wisdom and business strategy dictate that the marketing plan should always be thought through from the beginning. It can always be revised and improved, such as a business plan, but growth is hindered without it. The marketing plan will help set the appropriate values and allow you to think clearly.

Discuss important things with your team, and follow up later. You should also consider jotting the pointers down and summarizing the points to incorporate them in your marketing plan, if possible and appropriate.

It is after this initial exercise that you should use some of the following questions to write a paragraph, if possible, and summarize the important aspects of your marketing plan; you can begin by asking yourself what features are offered by your product or service. This will allow you to eventually identify the physical attributes of your product or service. Any other relevant features, such as what it does or how it differs from your competitors' offerings, will become evident.

Just like your imagination, your marketing activities are limitless, and this is what will allow your marketing plan to be diverse too. The marketing plan includes almost everything related to your product or service's advertising and promotion. This is crucial because an organized and validated plan will ensure success.[24]

It will also allow you to avoid any random and unplanned campaigns to advertise your product or service. Your aim, through a plan, should allow for the smooth execution of the marketing activities. The aim is to communicate the message that you would like to send about your products or services.

Begin by finalizing your product. Identify the product or service that you will offer, how it will stand out from those offered by the existing competition, and what will allow people to be interested in buying it.

Once the product is identified, figure out the price. It will be a bit difficult to do, so initially, a pricing strategy will come in handy. A strategy will eventually

---

[24]Matthew Podolsky, Preparing A Great Marketing Section For Your Business Plan, Forbes. November 19, 2019.
https://www.forbes.com/sites/theyec/2019/11/19/preparing-a-great-marketing-section-for-your-business-plan/?sh=5ed61cb32844

allow you to answer what volume to achieve to maximize sales and profits.[25]

Once the product basics are dealt with, you can continue to figure out the marketplace. Where will you be selling your product or service? Depending on your product type and its industry, the pricing and location will vary. Inexpensive, running items or services do not require a fancy location and vice versa.

The next part — advertising and sales — is often the last and tied to the place or channel. Deciding how you will advertise will determine the type of campaign used and the execution. The packaging will also be important because it shows how a product or service will be presented, whether it will settle well with the channel used and marketed well or not.

The sales channel is the last remaining step toward understanding a product well. This step will help you identify the mode of sale — determining whether your product will be shipped directly to customers or sold at outlets. Whichever channel you select will mean whether you economically reach your target-audience or not.

The marketing portion of a business plan addresses how you will get people to buy your product or service in sufficient quantities to make your

---

[25] Ibid.

business profitable. It consists of a lot of other factors, but one of the foremost are marketing analysis and strategy.

Market analysis, which assesses the market environment in which you compete, helps identify your competitors and analyze the strengths and weaknesses in your product or service.[26] It equips you to identify and quantify your target market. Marketing strategy, on the other hand, aims to document how you will differentiate your business from your competitors' business and what approach you will take to get customers to buy from you.

A sales plan is also a small part of the marketing plan. An integral component of any business plan is a strategy for getting your product or service to your targeted customers. There are many ways to reach your customers.

Marketing and sales plans often work together and frame the nature and timing of your marketing activities. The sales element is there to support tangible sales targets. These plans usually include a calendar that ties marketing and sales activities to

---

[26] Susan Ward, The Marketing Plan Section of the Business Plan, The Balance. January 16, 2020.
https://www.thebalancemoney.com/writing-the-business-plan-section-5-2947030

important operational events, such as a product launch or a public holiday.[27]

For instance, an advertising campaign may begin a few months before a new product is ready to be sold. As the date for the product's introduction approaches, advertisement activities will be stepped up. Once the new product hits the market, additional advertising is used to continue to support specific sales objectives.

Unique Selling Point (USP)

After you have identified your target audience and market, then ask one of the fundamental questions: *'How will your product or service distinguish itself and benefit the customer?'* This is an important question because the pricing and marketing can come later. If you can't understand your product well and how it can attract your target audience, then you will also be unable to sell and market it well.

The crucial point to note here is that a USP can be anything unique to a product or service. It should be anything justifiable and presentable.[28] It should be of

---

[27] Ibid.
[28] CFI Team, Marketing Plan Corporate Financing Institute, March 23, 2023.
https://corporatefinanceinstitute.com/resources/management/marketing-plan/

use to your audience, and the benefit to you is that it can be anything, either intangible and/or tangible.

The example of a cleaning product can help clarify what a USP is. Imagine a scenario where you are selling a fragrant spray that will allow your customers to keep their shoes clean and bacteria-free. The added benefit will be that your customers will not feel ashamed of taking their shoes off since there won't be a need to worry about odor.

This is a simple example, but a product has potentially many benefits that can be revealed through brainstorming. Once you do so, you can then prioritize the benefits and emphasize those that can potentially attract your customers the most. Your marketing plan will become effective, and you will only need to concentrate on the execution of the marketing.

In other words, a USP is what distinguishes your product from the competition and communicates it to your customers to become interested in your product or service. This is what forms the core of your marketing plan because everything is related to it.

There are several notable USPs that have helped products and services distinguish themselves and become famous. In fact, some of the most famous brands are known mostly because of the catchphrases that define their product.

KFC defines its products as "*finger-lickin' good,*" which they are, and that is how it became different from its competitor. Similarly, Domino's — the famous pizza chain — markets its pizza as one that will be delivered within thirty minutes. Even though their product is pizza, their main USP allows them to stand out, and it is only related to how they deliver the product. Their claim to fame is that they deliver hot and fresh pizzas in under thirty minutes. Otherwise, you will have them for free.

The famous airline Emirates distinguishes its flights as comfortable and around the world. This is what led them to make their slogan "Fly Emirates, Keep Discovering."

Even though all airlines carry passengers to their destinations, Emirates stood out and focused on providing more destinations and comfort than their competition.

This now leads us to the other elements of your marketing plan that need to be considered: pricing and strategy.

The USPs help define a strategy and allow businesses to focus on certain aspects, such as what Domino's Pizza or Emirates did. They determined that their USPs will come at a price, and how they will make customers pay for it is the strategy.

Pricing Strategy

The strategy to market your plan is often what drives the price of a product or service. After all, you will have to charge something reasonable and competitive. Otherwise, your competition will be the one benefitting and earning a profit. Your pricing strategy will help you determine the range of profit for your product.[29]

While you are free to charge what you may want, it mostly works for luxury or tailored goods and services. So, you will need to consider your industry sector and do research on your competitors' pricing to determine your product's possible price range.

This will help you answer what price to charge your customers since it is one of the most concerning questions for small business owners and new entrepreneurs. You will also need to determine the baseline price for your product, which is often known as penetration pricing, and it is one of the lowest possible prices for your product or service.

This is an essential piece of information to know because it will help you establish yourself as a new player, attract customers, and create market share. You can calculate it by summing up all your direct and indirect costs. You will also be able to estimate how

---

[29] Ibid.

competitive your product or service is and how well the price fares with that of your competition.

After you know the minimum price, you can add a fair share of profits so that your customer enjoys the price. This is a useful strategy because you will already know the price at which you will be able to do a breakeven. An analysis of your competitors' prices will guide you toward the fair market value of your product and allow you to determine how high you can reasonably go with the prices in the medium run.

Marketing Strategy

The matter pertaining to price, promotion, place, and product becomes clear in the marketing plan due to the element of strategy. The marketing strategy allows you to plan an approach to take to provide products or services to your customers. It allows you to set objectives and vision, just like how you do in an overall business plan.

An overall assessment and target allow you to estimate your sales and marketing targets. For instance, you may want to project how many customers you would like to reach, etc. The point of the marketing plan is to let anyone understand what you aim to do with your business at a glance so the strategy can be made accordingly.

The goals and features in a marketing strategy, as part of a marketing plan, will be as follows:

- Identifying your target audience
- Highlighting your market segment
- Understanding why your product or service is unique
- Knowing what drives pricing
- Researching market
- Having current and long-term plans

The four marketing Ps —product, price, promotion, and place — come together in the marketing strategy and help you define it. This is why it is important to clearly define and understand the Ps. It is the job of an entrepreneur to think these through and set them straight.[30]

For instance, the marketing plan can also include the different advertising types you will deploy and their timings. The marketing plan takes the marketing strategy that you developed to a tactical level. This will allow you to take the next steps to ensure that your product or service reaches a

---

[30] James Chen, What Is a Marketing Plan? Types and How to Write One, Investopedia.com. April 28, 2023.
https://www.investopedia.com/terms/m/marketing-plan.asp

customer and is sold. Timelines for the strategy and the steps are provided.

For example, how will you advertise your business? If you decide on radio ads, which stations will you choose, and at what times of day will you run ads? Can you afford enough repetition of the ad to make it memorable? How will you assess whether you're getting your money's worth from the radio spots?

The pricing strategy you outline in your marketing plan will answer the questions about costs and profits. This is where the marketing strategy will come into play. Ultimately, your business will become more competitive than before.[31]

Market Analysis

So now that we have mentioned market analysis, you may ask how you will even be able to determine if there is enough gap in the market for you to enter. This will help you understand and figure out the price that you will require to maintain a certain level of profit. To be able to answer these questions, you will need to perform a market analysis to have a robust marketing plan.

The market analysis presents your conclusions regarding external market factors that will affect

---

[31] Ibid.

your business. It examines the totality of the business environment in which you will compete.

Topics addressed in the market analysis include the existence and type of competitors, the characteristics of your target customers, market size, distribution costs, trends in your industry, and the market in general. Much of the information that will be included in the market analysis will be derived directly from the SWOT analysis that you performed early in the planning process.[32] The purpose of the market analysis is to set the stage for presenting your marketing strategy. That strategy sets forth your plan for successfully competing in your selected market.

Distribution Plan and Methods

After you have determined what forms your market and audience, you will need to figure out how your marketing and sales are going to be conducted. There are three main ways to distribute your product or service, but these three channels may not be applicable to your business, and these are mail, delivery, and website. In some cases, you may employ sales representatives to reach your customers.

---

[32] CFI Team, Marketing Plan Corporate Financing Institute, March 23, 2023.
https://corporatefinanceinstitute.com/resources/management/marketing-plan/

So, how will you determine which mode to utilize? It will also depend on whether your product or service creation is direct or not — whether it can directly go from production to consumer or involve a retailer in between. The best way to identify the mode of distribution is to make a list of all steps involved, from production to sale.

The next question to answer will be related to the cost of distribution to figure out the best-suited modes for your product or service.

How much time do you require, and how much time does each method take? Your product's packaging and handling might also dictate how you display, package, and sell your product or service.

Also, incorporate regulations pertaining to labeling and anything that goes along with it. Once this is set, you can determine the levels of inventory that you need to hold, as per the minimum level of sales, and ensure a smooth execution of orders.

Once your distribution mode is set, you can figure out whether your sale plan will include any warranties and discounts; how will these be ensured, and what conditions will need to be maintained for fulfillment? Lastly, the distribution plan should also include delivery charges of all sorts, including penalties and terms of service agreement.

Sales Strategy

Once your distribution plan is set, you can delegate this to the sales team and ensure the strategy is aligned. The sales strategy will highlight what type of salespersons will be employed and their responsibilities. From those making sales calls to demonstrating and selling products, their requirements need to be assessed to ensure that sales are conducted effectively and that their efficiency is reviewed.

All compensation and benefits need to be highlighted. Lastly, it needs to be clarified if there would be a training program for the sales teams, and this will form part of the marketing plan.

Advertising Plan

This section deals with how you will be promoting your product and delivering its USP. There will be a need to identify the promotional avenues that are available for your product. This is why it is important to remain focused on your USPs and identify the appropriate advertising and marketing strategies. Most importantly, finalize what message you want your target audience to receive.

The approach to adopt in this case is to ensure effective media that are relevant to your product or service. Know which medium will be the most effective and how it will affect your advertising budget. You need to set an annual budget and divide it according to each medium. If possible, allocate percentages to each medium to direct your teams.

The media that is available to you is wide but includes the following: website, social media, post-mail, flyers, partner advertising, radio, magazines, directories, billboards, bus/train stations, and television.

Other than setting a budget, you should also estimate how much revenue will be brought in because of the promotions. When possible, try to utilize promotional plans such as samples, coupons, reward points, etc.

If your industry involves a trade show, you can also use it to promote your products and tap sales opportunities. Having a plan in place and in your calendar will allow your sales and promotion teams to align well and be prepared from before.

Similarly, other avenues of publicity can be utilized to seek opportunities, such as the use of social media to engage with consumers and collaborate with relevant industries or partner organizations.

Conclusion

The challenge in developing an effective marketing plan is to select effective and appropriate sales and distribution channels. If your business is small enough that you can directly intervene, then you should try to provide the services and seek feedback from your customers.

Your participation in the sales process will be quite fruitful and rewarding. Also, just like a business plan, it is important to remember that no business is too small to have a marketing plan. If you have a product and a market, then your business size will not really matter to your customers. All you need to do is prove that you have something unique and valuable to offer.

The marketing plan details the strategy that a business will utilize to advertise its products to its customers. The plan will allow your business to perform sales and promotion effectively. Your business and marketing objectives will be aligned, and teams will be able to perform well.

The important aspect of a marketing plan is also how promotion and sales are assessed. The metrics highlighted will ensure that your business will be effective in its strategy and adopt relevant initiatives. Having a marketing plan should not mean that everything is fixed. The marketing plan should be flexible and adjusted as your business progresses and the environment changes. The metrics for performance evaluation will allow you to have performance measured at a glance. You will understand which areas need to be concentrated on and which do not require as much attention.

Chapter 14: Affiliate Marketing Plan

When marketing for your products these days, online marketing is the go-to option for most businesses because it allows you to find and connect with your potential clientele. Companies can launch campaigns worth tens of thousands of dollars online to market their products or services; however, the budgets can be tight for startups and small enterprises. To utilize small budgets and to do so efficiently, businesses often engage with affiliate marketers since the returns on investment are high and easily measurable.

Affiliate marketers can be professional bloggers, copywriters, and social media influencers. They often have either a blog or a website on a subject and market segment that allows them to have a substantial following. According to Statista, affiliate marketing in the U.S. was an industry worth over eight billion dollars in 2022, while Influencer Marketing Hub estimates that the number will nearly double in 2024.[33]

---

[33] J.G. Navarro, Affiliate Marketing Spending, Statista. January 6, 2023.
https://www.statista.com/statistics/693438/affiliate-marketing-spending/
Werner Geyser, Affiliate Marketing Report, Influencer Marketing Hub. March 28, 2023.
https://influencermarketinghub.com/affiliate-marketing-report/

How it often works is that an affiliate link or coupon code is generated that is shared with the followers of the promoter. This easily allows the companies to assess how many clicks were generated or times a coupon code was successful. This ties in with how much revenue is brought forth by an affiliate marketing scheme and can be compared with other marketers or another strategy.

While it does seem simple enough and risk-free, when compared to expensive marketing options, it is still important to match your market segment when considering an affiliate marketer. They can often have a wide variety of followers, so the process of selecting an affiliate should be done carefully and with the help of data analysis of their followers to maximize the reach of the product.

Generating Leads

Since affiliate marketing pertains to the promotion of products based on commissions when people buy those products, it is important to create trust to convince your audience to buy a product. This will come through quality assurance and support. The ability to portray your organization as an authority in the field and to provide accurate information goes a long way in generating leads.

Your audience needs to be respected, not considered fools. They should be seen as those willing to buy something of value and interest to them. This is why narrowing down your niche to an underserved segment will prove to be the most valuable and loyal following of your product or service.

The second thing to remember is not to pay too heavily so as to compromise on your profits and the product's inherent value. The commission rates should correspond with the sales volume to make commercial sense and reach enough customers to create a cult following. Digital and niche products can have high commission rates, but this does not have to mean that you get less out of your affiliate, and the deal should be respectful of your interests.

Affiliates have creative ways to reach your audience segment. One way this can be done is by paying for product reviews or 'unboxings' to assess how your product is perceived. This will help you engage well with the customers and receive their feedback.

Slowly and steadily, you will be able to understand generating leads is quite significant through detailed reviews and expert or celebrity endorsements. Primarily, this helps establish your product's legitimacy and allows you to engage with your audience. Eventually, you will be able to ascertain which form of online communication and social media platform they prefer and what they are most interested in.

Ultimately, leads boil down to the value that you can create through your product or service and how well it can be communicated with your audience. The key is to have content that can be engaging since this is what converts leads into sales. Businesses prioritize sales, and this is their mistake.

With access to the internet, information, and social media, customers are quite aware these days, and they can differentiate between a sales pitch that provides them value versus one that does not. If there is no value, then the customer might not consider your product or service ever again.

Creating Perception and Value

When trying to promote a product or a service through affiliates, you should be clear about what message you would like to be communicated by a marketer. This will drive the perception and value of your brand. The first thing to do so will be to think from the perspective of a potential customer.

Consider what your audience may be searching for and what may appear of interest to them. Through this step, you can try to answer their questions and present a solution to them. This will show how your product or service might be of use to them.

Clear and useful tips through your product or service can also be another strategy to persuade customers to finalize a sale. This will allow you to avoid direct sales pitches, which can be aided through the use of 'calls to action.' These are prompts with discounts or promotional codes to encourage your customers to try or purchase a product.

The actions can vary from *try now* to *buy now, pay later,* etc. These actions are links that lead to a landing page that showcases key features in an innovative way to encourage customers to make a purchase. Similarly, any reviews should discuss how the products can be purchased.

A Growing Industry

Affiliate marketing has garnered the attention of investors because their platforms have raised an all-time high of one and a half billion dollars in 2022.[34] As of 2021, the affiliate-related marketing industry had grown by over twenty-fix percent, and firms have reached ten thousand.[35] Amazon Associates holds the most power, with over twenty percent market share and the interest in affiliate marketing booming.

Through affiliate marketing, a company can gain unique insights into what people are for a specific audience. You should create a product that aims to fill a market gap rather than just follow profitability. For

---

[34] Ibid.
[35] Ibid.

successful marketing, customers should receive value, and you will receive a following.

For a successful product, try to create added services or related products to tap into the market rather than to upsell or trick customers into buying. This will provide you with an extra stream of income and allow you to leverage the power of affiliate sales in your market segment.

Since maintaining contact with an audience is the primary aim, newsletters, email marketing, and reviews are the most used strategies to help highlight your product and allow customers to purchase it. These days, a viral video can channel thousands of dollars to be earned in less than a day.

This will allow you to connect with your market segment and those who relate to your values. If anything, a successful affiliate marketing campaign will pay off for itself and perhaps why it is a growing marketing domain. Utilizing affiliates also allows you to be on top of trends and marketing tricks that can provide your brand and marketing team with a refresher course.

These days, marketing is all about understanding algorithms and trends. What your audience thinks can be changed as your brand's perception changes, and all these things are easily tracked through the use of 'cookies'. Websites utilize these forms of often non-invasive cyber trackers to keep a check on visitors and customers alike.

For instance, it is crucial for you to distinguish who bought using your affiliate marketer versus who did not and what their behavior was online. You may be able to ascertain how much each customer paid, how much time they took to finalize a purchase, and what products or services they were most interested in.

These 'cookies' have crucial data on customers that are anonymized these days and allow you to understand purchase patterns. This means that you have an insight into your customers, and you can take the most advantage out of your affiliate marketing campaign through other means of online marketing.

Finally, experienced professionals and organizations will always help you stay ahead of the trend. They can help you avoid pitfalls and wrong decisions that can cost you a fortune and time too. All this has made affiliate marketing an effective and viable strategy for small-to-medium enterprises.

Types of Affiliate Marketing

Now that it has been made clear why affiliate marketing is important, it should also be known that there are several forms of it, though there are three main types that I would like to discuss in this chapter.

Launching Campaigns

The most common form of marketing that is readily available deals with launching simple campaigns on social media platforms. These campaigns can be simple to set up, requiring little to no expertise; however, they can be costly and time-consuming if done blindly and by inexperienced individuals. The strategy aims to target any niche based solely on age or location, and it is referred to as unattached affiliate marketing.

This is often used when it is difficult to connect with customers, so a single-platform or medium approach is used to promote a product or service. Newcomers are often found in the domain, and they utilize blogs, social media accounts, or a single platform to conduct the marketing. This means that affiliate marketing is not attached to your market segment.

Related Affiliate Marketing

This leads us to the second common type — related affiliate marketing. As the name suggests, it is more related to your target audience than unrelated affiliate marketing. Marketers promote the links to their audience and often do so through links, banners, or text.

This form of marketing frequently includes related products that may be slightly affiliated with a segment; however, the product or service may not have been tested or reviewed in reality. This is why it poses a serious risk to the brand because the customer experience may be entirely unexpected. The lack of focus and reliability also means that the quality is only as advertised, and the responsibility would rely upon you or the manufacturer.

As a result, there is a danger of losing the audience's trust and brand image. This can be beneficial if the product or service is of or related to an established brand in order for the audience to safely embrace it and for the campaign to be successful.

Affiliate Marketing

Finally, this leads us to affiliate marketing. It is exactly the opposite of unattached affiliate marketing since it is not just about accumulating a reach or maximizing sales. The number of clicks, for instance, on the affiliate's promotion is not a priority.

An affiliate often tests a product with complete fairness and honesty. They may or may not like the product, but they will try to give their true impressions and honest feedback. Unboxing can be considered the classic example of involved affiliate marketing. This is because the affiliates would tell people whether or not they might continue to use the product or service and if they would recommend it to their followers.

The drawbacks of this segment maybe if a product or service is too generic and competitive. In the case of a cola drink or cleaning service, the difference from the competition might be too vague or indistinguishable, and it might be difficult to ascertain a quality that people may like or not since it may be subjective. This is why it is important to understand which type of affiliate marketing would need to be utilized.

As a result, there is a danger of losing the audience's trust and brand image. This can be beneficial if the product or service is of or related to an established brand in order for the audience to safely embrace it and the campaign to be successful.

Involved Affiliate Marketing

Finally, this leads us to involved affiliate marketing. This is exactly the opposite of unattached affiliate marketing since it is not just about accumulating a reach or maximizing sales. The number of clicks, for instance, on the affiliate's promotion is not a priority.

An affiliate often tests a product with complete fairness and honesty. They may or may not like the product, but they will try to give their true impressions and honest feedback. Unboxing can be considered a classic example of involved affiliate marketing. This is because the affiliates would tell people whether or not they might continue to use the product or service and if they would recommend it to their followers. The drawbacks of this segment maybe if a product or service is too generic and competitive. In the case of a cola drink or cleaning service, the difference from the competition might be too vague or indistinguishable, and it might be difficult to ascertain a quality that people may like or not since it may be subjective. This is why it is important to understand which type of affiliate marketing would need to be utilized.

Conclusion

Considering the low-cost and low-risk nature of affiliate marketing, it is no wonder that it is an extremely effective mode of marketing, and what needs to be considered is what type may be utilized. It is quite profitable for both the advertiser and the marketer. It is also engaging because results can be easily measured compared to conventional forms of marketing.

Also, creativity and marketing efforts can be used over a longer period of time since they cost much less than other forms of marketing. The added benefit to small and medium enterprises is that they can gain the attention that they require and receive a significant boost in sales. The flexibility and scalability of affiliate marketing are what have led interest in it to spike along with a high return on investment. This is because the enterprise is only responsible for paying per click or banner. This can prove to be a cost-effective measure, especially if the target audience is wide.

Also, the affiliate is responsible for all marketing so the enterprise can focus on the analysis of data, conventional marketing, and improving the product or service. The presence of commission-based sales in affiliate marketing also means that leads, or at least reach, are almost certain, and this is why it is a perfect form of marketing for small-to-medium enterprises.

With increasing competition and interest in affiliate marketing, technology is advancing, which leads to better results and insights. What is required, though, is enough research and interest to ascertain what type of affiliate marketing strategy to adopt. Like any strategy, it requires much planning and oversight in order for the campaign to be effective. As a result, an effective affiliate marketing program necessitates some planning. The terms and conditions must be clearly stated, particularly if the contract agreement compensates for traffic rather than sales, as affiliate marketing has the potential for fraud as well.

Chapter 15: Social Media Marketing Plan

Businesses used to have detailed marketing plans laid out for a year in advance at times. There was a lot of emphasis on copywriting and creativity. These days, it is now easier and simpler than ever to connect with people, and it is all due to technology.

The credit goes to the internet and social media, although this means that marketing success relies on an understanding of social media and its trends these days. The benefits of social media marketing are absurdly evident since there are over four and a half billion registered social media users, and people have spent over twelve and a half trillion hours online in 2022! [36]

This means that the average time spent online is roughly two hours and twenty minutes per person every day. An average person uses over eight platforms in any given month.[37] The major growth in social media usage has been witnessed in TikTok, YouTube, and Instagram.

With ample opportunities and avenues to market and grow, you need to be focused and have clearly

---

[36] Kepios, Digital 2022 Global Overview Report, Kepios, Hootsuite and We Are Social. 2022.
https://datareportal.com/reports/digital-2022-global-overview-report

[37] Ibid.

defined, as well as realistic, objectives. The failure to direct your energy could mean a loss of both energy and time. Otherwise, all your energy and investment could be lost.

This is why this book emphasizes planning. It is simple and easy to succeed when you follow clearly defined and realistic objectives. So, one needs to strategize on social media marketing and plan everything accordingly.

Social Media Strategy

Similar to your business or marketing strategy, a social media strategy is where you outline your goals and define the tactics that you may utilize to achieve them. You will also need to highlight the key performance indicators that you would like to use to track your marketing performance.

The best thing about social media strategy is that it is one of the simplest and easiest aspects to design and implement in a business. The improved technology means that your plans can be tangible and measurable. Social media platforms have a lot of information on their users these days, and this can be used to target a specific audience segment.

The best part about social media marketing is that it will provide you with the engagement and reach that your business requires. This is because social media platforms are all based on algorithms that market and prioritize content based on a variety of factors. Your brand awareness will improve over time with consistent marketing.

In order to run successful social media campaigns, it is important that your strategy is based on ample research and clear targets. The first thing that you can begin with is identifying which platform you will be utilizing to reach your target audience. All you need is initial marketing successes, and the nature of social media propels your brand's presence thereafter.

If anyone understands brand management, then this should be fairly simple to follow. The longer your brand is visible, the more it will reach your audience and eventually lead to higher engagement and sales. With online marketplaces and avenues to sell products, you can replicate success quite successfully and quickly online.

There are some hidden benefits that social media marketing provides that you can use to tailor your campaigns while improving brand perception and management at the same time. The first thing is that you will generate more leads, which will mean more money and traffic on your social media pages and website than before. You will be able to personalize the content and promote it.

The better your campaigns are, the more chances you will have of creating content that goes viral. You will be able to also provide increased customer support and service online than before. If there is any interesting or eye-raising idea, then you can promote it as a challenge or ask a social-media influencer to help with your content.

The ability to measure metrics, perform analysis in real-time, and conduct time-series analysis are some of the most useful benefits of having a social-media campaign. This will lead you to revise your social media strategy as you learn and your brand grows. Since social media is present all around us, it has become a necessity for businesses to engage with it.

Planning

With so many social media platforms and global audiences, your opportunities are endless, but there is one thing that you can do to engage, influence, and convert your target audience.

With the basics of social media dealt with, you need to learn how to plan a social media strategy and how to execute it. The primary thing is that your social media content should align with your strategy. Some simple steps can help you plan out a social media strategy.

First thing: With all business planning — define your goals as mentioned earlier. Your goals will determine your strategy. It will help you answer what you and your business want to achieve.

For instance, would you like to increase engagement and awareness or overall sales? If sales are your focus, then you will need to plan out lead generation. You will also need to understand marketing and business goals may be a bit different since the former focuses on promotion rather than profit generation.

So, it is important to set your priorities and plan your strategy to understand how each of your goals will require a different plan. Setting goals will always mean that you have assigned key indicators that will be compared against social media metrics. Different platforms may require you to set different metrics. A simple example is that Facebook has reach and engagement as the key things to focus on, although Instagram is mainly about brand interaction and discovery. [38]

All this means that you will need to monitor and tweak metrics quite often to manage your content and its reach. This will mean the difference between your targets and achievements on social media. The next

---

[38] Ibid.

thing to do would be to conduct ample research on your audience and content.

Research and Competitive Analysis

So, how will you plan and execute a social media strategy when you do not know how to personalize your content to appeal to your audience? This requires messages and content to understand how your audience is and what they might appreciate or not. Conducting thorough research through surveys, interviews, and market research is the key in this regard.

You may also try to conduct focus groups or use insights from community forums and professionals. There are also a lot of online platforms that provide you with data analysis and strategy, such as BuzzSomo, HootSuite, etc.

The important thing here is that some of the online services will help you understand your target audience and advice on how to set up online marketing campaigns. At the end of the day, you want to know who your customers are and what attracts them. Even a basic knowledge of insights and demographics can be enough to have a decent start and avoid common mistakes.

If you feel like you need to know more than you do, then feel free to research about your industry and competitors. This is a similar tactic that you utilize in finding and creating a product. If anything, your information and comprehension of your audience will be refreshed.

A closer inspection of the industry will also allow you to learn how to perceive your customers. This will certainly help in your endeavor to campaign on different platforms and create successful campaigns.

Research will help you find out how to curate messaging and what type of content appeals to your audience. At times, the frequency and timings of posts might help, too, but it varies depending on the platform and region. Eventually, you will begin to tap into the instincts of your audience.

Platform

The strategy and research will boil down to which platform(s) you choose to engage with your audience. Instagram is the trendiest and most used platform, with an algorithm that spreads and markets products the most. Consequently, marketing is also competitive and relatively expensive, but the return on investment is high for products and services that are available online.

With social media platforms from TikTok, Instagram, Facebook, WhatsApp, Twitter, YouTube, LinkedIn, etc., it can be confusing to narrow down to a platform or two. Your research will help you narrow down to a few options. It will not be a wise strategy to all out and utilize every platform.

Not only is it difficult to manage multiple platforms, especially for small-to-medium enterprises, but it is also not viable. Each platform has a unique feature that sets it apart from the competition but allows you to engage in a different manner.

For example, YouTube and Facebook are all about live engagement and detailed posts that are aided with pictures or videos. Twitter, on the other hand, is about microblogging and professional posts. Instagram and TikTok are about viral and motivational content through the use of visual content — short videos and picture-based content.

Execution

Finally, it will boil down to how you thought things through and executed everything that sets a successful campaign apart from others. The main aspect to highlight on social media is to set the right tone.

You should know that each brand and profile on social media eventually adopts a tone. You should identify yours and see how you would interact with the world. Is your content going to be professional or casual?

You can decide to engage in humor and puns or not at all. The way you set the tone decides how much you engage with your audience. It will also depend on how you would like to present your brand's personality — is it fresh and inclusive or simply restrictive?

Your tone will decide what theme your content takes. The next thing is scheduling and evaluation. This will make your life easy and allow you to test your strategies and optimize your content. Tweaking and changing things until you crack it is how a brand's image will be built online.

It will take some time, regardless of how established your brand is.

Schedule Your Content

It can be difficult to keep up with the pace of social media, and if you post regularly, keeping to a schedule is important for consistency. There is no perfect or one-shoe-fits-all strategy. The main thing to do is optimize content and remain vigilant.

Another aspect of execution is creating avenues of engagement and driving campaigns with your online community. An active online brand will mean that its community is engaged and aware of any products or services and related activities. If people have questions, then it is important that they are answered.

Any complaints should never be avoided. Instead, try to respond empathetically, positively, and professionally. Creating an engaging community also means to keep them happy. Occasionally, some brands conduct polls or informal questions to know more about their audience.

Engage your community by asking questions through polls or surveys. It makes them feel a part of the community, but it also may help you find out more about your customer base. Paid advertising in between will help promote your product and keep it relevant to your audience.

Cross-channel and collaborative marketing can also be conducted on social media. It will be difficult to execute, but the results are often rewarding. Eventually, your goal should be to remain focused on the goals.

Think S.M.A.R.T

So now that we know about goal-setting and the basics of social media, how will you set them and ensure that they achieve your objectives? You may have wondered about ways to have clear and concise objectives on a timeline.

For this, you have to adopt a S.M.A.R.T. approach, which is about specificity, measurability, achievability, relevance, and timing. This will help you think things through and align your priorities. This is a technique to help you clearly design, evaluate, and plan success.[39]

The result is an approach that eliminates chances of having random and guesswork. The clarity removes space for uninformed and general decisions. You will be able to define and track progress and milestones.

The SMART approach allows for realistic and tangible targets. You are able to decide what you aim to achieve, how it will be done, and in how much time. This is important because it functions as a checklist of sorts in the daily routine.

The end results are a focus and not the process. This helps avoid having too many things to do but nothing to gauge and assess the progress against. Since everything is specified, you get to answer who gets to make certain choices, what they are, and where your goals will be assessed.

---

[39] Kimberlee Leonard, Rob Watts, The Ultimate Guide To S.M.A.R.T. Goals, Forbes. May 4, 2022.
For further reading and a guide on S.M.A.R.T., visit the following link: https://www.forbes.com/advisor/business/smart-goals/

Managers will be able to ascertain if goals are realistic or not through this strategy. Any hurdles in the way will be identified and worked on to achieve the goal. This will also provide your workforce with measurements to be included in the action plan.

Anything required for performance evaluation will be clearly indicated, and success will be measured accordingly. The ability to discuss and finalize measurability is also something that will allow for realistic performance and input of your employees. This also paves the way for achievability and relevance.

Conclusion

Once you finalize and go through the SMART aspects, you will be able to efficiently complete projects and set realistic deadlines. Finally, with the help of a social media strategy and SMART technique, you will able to ascertain the important questions that can lead you to success.

If you are still wondering if it may be too much, then follow a simple exercise and ask yourself the questions below. They will help you create an effective social media strategy and understand everything that has been discussed in this chapter. Even if you do follow everything, the following questions will enable you to conduct a realistic and thorough evaluation of your strategy:

- How effective is your social media strategy?
- What do you think seems to be working for your business, and what is not?
- Who is your target audience?
- Who is engaging with you?
- Which social media platforms do you use to engage with your audience?
- How is your social media presence different from that of your competition?

You should also try to always know and ask the following things about your target audience:

- Age
- Location
- Average income
- Typical job title or industry
- Interests

Chapter 16: Community-based Marketing Plan

With the spread in the use of social media, there are a lot of opportunities to market your brand and increase its presence through online communities. The increase in internet usage and time spent on social media means that connecting with your audience has become easy and important. This means that it is essential for brands to have a community-based marketing plan if they are to increase awareness and connect with their audience.

This type of marketing has picked up pace over the past two decades as advertising is personalized and two-way, unlike conventional forms of marketing. Community-based marketing plans allow businesses to interact with the intended audience and build relationships with them. There are diverse ways to advertise through communities, such as through local events and sponsorships.

Every business can grow the visibility of its brands through this method and utilize numerous channels to create value for the community. People appreciate the participation of brands on a local level. This improves the reach of the business and provides a chance for a brand to engage with the audience and understand what they hold important.

For instance, a rural town's farmer's market can be tapped to support the community and promote their interests. Charity drives and fundraisers can also be set up to improve engagement with the target audience. This will also create content for your brand's online presence that can be shared on social media.

Community engagement is viewed positively since it establishes the legitimacy and ability of the brand to associate with their audience. This helps build trust through a personal connection that can lead to sustainable business over time. It will also lead you to identify themes and interests that may be associated with a certain community and its geographical locality.

A Brand Strategy

Community-based marketing is what aims to bring people together around a product or service and drive them through a purpose, providing insights accordingly. The relationships that are created with prospects and customers alike help drive the strategies that strengthen an organization's value.

The strategies entail bringing people together and providing a higher purpose for the community. The wholesome feeling is what also highlights a product, allowing an organization to stand out among the competition. The engagement and sense of purpose make brands understand their market segment and help them remain connected.

Marketers essentially focus on turning communities into gateways to their marketplaces. The key focus is to tap some of the major benefits of community marketing, such as targeting the audience, making connections, and customizing messages over time that can lead to growth for a brand.

The best way to understand the purpose of the strategy is to gain an understanding of what the targeted audience might be like with the 'community' as a sample size. This means that messages can be repurposed to suit marketing plans. The personalization allows engagement to be value-driven rather than number-driven.

Benefits

The target audience can be easily understood through community-based marketing. The 'soft power' that comes with this means that sponsoring groups and teams for events will provide the trust and connection that every brand requires. Some startups create their marketing strategies around community-based marketing.

Organizations such as AirBnB, AIG, Dyson, Revolut, and Uber have grown exponentially. They have focused on attracting a huge number of customers through community building. Over time, they let their values lead their audience to understand their needs.

Being present and engaging with your audience is the key. This requires long-term commitment, perhaps through sponsorship of local events, charity drives, or holiday galas. The customer base that is engaged through community-based marketing is loyal. This leads to organic growth and marketing through 'word-of-mouth.'

It is one of the most rewarding and least expensive strategies that can be gained through community-based marketing. The key is like that in social-media marketing, which is to choose an appropriate market segment. The brand's values and community engagement will resonate accordingly. If a company is keen on targeting a specific city, then this is why popular sporting events are either sponsored or a presence is built on recurring events.

This leads to an engagement with the target audience and their families. This can be expensive and requires targeted planning, which also means the use of expert resources that small businesses might not have. The benefit for them is that they can concentrate on their audience rather than market using conventional marketing strategies that are indirect and certainly cannot provide quick returns.

Investment into building a community also means that communication is a two-way process. Key elements such as aspirations, feedback, and desire can be understood. It is not something that can be gained through other marketing strategies. A business can achieve this goal by engaging with the audience and gathering insights through data and feedback.

If a brand wants to establish a presence or grow further, then it can also boost its marketing through influencers in a community. The best part about this is that these individuals can be local leaders, favorite coaches, or famous community members. Their personal repute means that engagement and brand marketing will be strong and value-based.

This is also important when a brand wants to highlight a value or relate it to a trait that community members may hold highly. This is an indirect form of marketing and understanding a community.

These investments can pay off quite well over time, such as the brand loyalty that is associated with specialized brands. The case of Harley Davidson is quite important because they promoted and catered to a specific community — bikers. They formed groups in every major city where they sold a certain number of bikes and held events to bring their 'community' together.

This has resulted in the company maintaining a strong brand presence and withstanding the challenges over time. It is now valued at around eight billion dollars. Their use of other marketing strategies is not primary, and this is what helps them grow. They remained concentrated.

Challenges

A Kantar study of over eleven thousand people has revealed that around eighty percent of customers want companies to help and increase engagement.[40] The study took place in twenty-one countries. It also helps explain why there is an increasing focus on 'customer first' and community-oriented marketing.

This reinforces the purpose of community-based marketing, which is to be focused and personalized as per the target audience. Customers want to be respected and heard. The brand values must resonate with their values and what they support.

This is why posts on social media are often taken down after a backlash or after an advertising campaign includes anything that people dislike. This means there must be a dedicated team and strategy for community-based marketing. The allocation of

---

[40] Kantar, Covid-19 Barometer, Kantar
https://www.kantar.com/campaigns/covid-19-barometer

resources and hiring of relevant staff can mean that it will be difficult for small businesses to catch up and engage systematically.

The required long-term commitment can be difficult for startups, too, although it can always be scaled. The benefits outweigh the costs and challenges. If anything, even a small community-based marketing strategy can mean that the insights will drive the values and improve strategies over time.

Appropriate customer experience and engagement will eventually convert a community into a loyal customer base. However, it is important to note that every strategy requires revision and evaluation over time. Surveys and questions can help provide reality checks, no matter how small or huge a business may be.

The low costs that are associated with customer acquisition will also mean that there is a need to keep the community engaged. Reliable community leaders and sources of information will help your organization to have a successful brand over time.

This is a strategy that can be cumbersome to market, time-consuming, and expensive to deploy because it requires expertise and an engagement team. This might not be feasible for low-value startups or organizations due to low revenue.

Tactics

Given the benefits, even small businesses should consider deploying some form of community-based marketing. This can be anything as small as providing gifts through random draws, quizzes, or games. This will help draw your audience and allow you to engage with them.

As an important marketing tactic, this is cost-effective, and it means that you can also use online platforms to engage in community marketing. The simplest thing to do is create a page for your product or service on an appropriate social media platform. This is also important because your social media presence will strengthen, and you will gain regular insights into your customer engagement through analytics and data.

As things progress, you can identify and decide to support a social cause that your target audience relates to or associates with. This can be through a kiosk at a carnival or a sponsorship of an event. It can be as small as a presence at a farmer's market if it lies in your market segment.

When things begin to grow or if you find a trend, then it can be important to support social issues and advocacy groups that relate to your brand's values and principles. Similarly, local leaders such as teachers or coaches can also be hired as advocates of a campaign or even an ambassador. This will allow your target audience to join and grow your community.

Eventually, your business's marketing strategy will include an aspect of community-building. The sooner you do, the less costly and more rewarding it will be in the long run. So, get started and reap the benefits!

Step 4: Cost Cutting System

Chapter 17: Importance of Cost Cutting

Once you are done planning the core business elements of your business, next up would be planning your cost-cutting strategies. You have to understand that every single penny saved counts, and it does make it worth a lot for startups and small businesses.

Since this book is about the roadmap to success, running a successful business requires you to keep the costs low, although this should translate to not too low and not too excessive cost cutting. There are some inevitable costs with any business, such as salaries, bills, sundry expenses, etc. Some of these costs, such as energy bills and salaries, increase over time and must be adjusted for inflation and other factors.

Less money spent will eventually mean more money available for you when you need it the most. This will translate into benefits for your business functions and administration to have a free cash flow. The problem is that you cannot cut down on all costs since some may be indirectly important, such as central air-conditioning or heating and pantry.

When you begin to differentiate what costs should be cut and what should remain, you will come to an understanding of cutting costs. So, what is the real importance of cost-cutting — other than the obvious

— you may wonder. It is due to the uncertainty that prevails in the financial and economic world.

You may wake up one day to find that the crude oil prices have jumped over ten dollars, interest rates have risen by a percent, or a natural calamity has affected your business. The effects can be direct or indirect, although the impact would be significant and noticeable. You do not want your cash flow or debts to increase due to a lack of planning, resulting in your inability to support your product prices and deliveries.

Understanding Cost Cutting

Cost cutting is any strategy or measure that aims to reduce costs in an organization to reduce expenses and improve profitability. The measures are usually implemented during a financially challenging time for a business and/or during an economic downturn. It can also be implemented in anticipation of a fall in profitability, so it may just be part of a business's strategy.

Maintaining profitability and efficiency can be a tricky thing to do for managers and entrepreneurs alike, although it is a necessary strategy to run a successful business. While it is an important thing to do, deciding which areas require cost reduction will inevitably mean having a detailed and intimate knowledge of how your business functions. The importance of cost-cutting becomes evident when we think about a business in the long run.

As your organization grows, the business functions will expand and lead to increased costs. This means that it is essential for organizations to periodically review costs and ensure cost efficiency. It will help you remain informed of costs and achieve your business goals in a systematic manner.

Other than management, the ultimate gain of low costs is the investors and shareholders in a business since profits will increase and lead to dividends on investments. In times of economic downturn, controlled costs will lead to consistency and survivability of the business and ease financial pressures. Having a keen eye on costs can mean the difference between success and failure since your management will be able to focus on a business's smooth functioning and growth.

While there are a lot of ways to cut costs, the measures taken will solely depend upon the circumstances and relevant strategy. From simply laying off employees to changing premises, businesses can deploy a range of strategies to reduce or eliminate costs. In some extreme cases where the costs are high, organizations can choose to downsize business functions and move to a smaller office compared to before and terminate third-party contracts and services.

In today's ever-changing world, the ability of a business to adjust to technology and implement effective industry solutions can be a huge cost or an alternative to cost-cutting. An organization may install a robot at an assembly to save on labor costs or deploy a specialized solution such as that of SAP to streamline supply-chain operations.

Accounting Systems in Cost-cutting Strategy

The way accounting and specialized software can help in cutting your costs can be quite rewarding along the way once you start to utilize them the right way. Harvard Business Review published some expert opinions that highlighted the benefits and ways of implementing a cost-cutting strategy. [41]

According to them, you have to look for ways to save on administrative costs first and remember the following two points:

Firstly, you should try to have all costs appropriated and calculated for. You should not expect to find a single solution that would drastically reduce your costs and solve your problem at once. This is the golden rule.

---

[41] Kevin Coyne, Shawn T. Coyne, and Edward J. Coyne, Sr, When You've Got to Cut Costs—Now, Harvard Business Review. May 2010.
Available online: https://hbr.org/2010/05/when-youve-got-to-cut-costs-now

The reason is that such a solution would probably be too risky for your organization to implement anyway. No one rule fits all. Instead, you should aim to achieve your goal with a mix of ten or more actions.

Secondly, the more you cut your costs, the more you will disrupt your organization. Therefore, you should match your cost-cutting ideas to your savings target. Small ideas with little impact on other departments can help you save up to 10% of costs. Bigger ideas that involve redesigning or reorganizing your work can eliminate low-value activities and save up to 20% of costs. But the biggest ideas that affect multiple departments or programs are usually needed when you want to save 30% or more, and they can cause the most organizational disruption.

You might wonder what is the real benefit of using software to calculate and assess your costs. It improves business efficiency because you get all your costs at a glance. You can, thereby, analyze the costs that are most common and changing over a selected period.

Finding and analyzing patterns can help you ascertain which business units are costing you a fortune or not. Cost accounting is vital for businesses to track and manage their costs effectively. It helps find and remove inefficiencies in business operations.

With the right cost accounting systems, you can identify which measures to deploy and what strategy to implement. Companies can witness where they are wasting money and develop strategies to reduce those costs accordingly. This helps set appropriate budgets and improves efficiency over the long run.

Benefits to Budgeting and Cost-comparison

Here are some of the additional benefits of cost accounting for your business efficiency. The first one is your product's cost because they matter the most at the end of the day. It dictates how efficient you are and how you compare to your industry.

This dictates how much revenue you bring and what your profitability may look like. Given that cost accounting enables the calculation of the total production costs of a product or service, you can also use software to analyze this data. You can identify the operations involved that increase your costs and reduce your inefficiency.

This data can help you improve your production process and boost your profits. Cost accounting is a useful tool for finding and eliminating business inefficiencies. It can help businesses in the following ways:

Set Realistic Budgets

Cost accounting helps businesses to set realistic budgets and forecast future costs accurately. By doing a comprehensive cost analysis, businesses can anticipate changes in production costs, market conditions, and customer demands and adjust their plans accordingly.

Identify Overhead Costs

Cost accounting enables businesses to analyze their fixed and variable overhead costs. This analysis can reveal any inefficiencies and potential areas of waste. The results can lead to cost-cutting measures that improve the bottom line.

Aid Decision-making

Cost accounting provides valuable information that supports businesses in making smart decisions. Businesses can choose which products to make, which suppliers to work with, and which production methods to use by examining costs. Knowing the costs associated with each process step can help businesses make more efficient decisions.

Activity-based Costing (ABC)

ABC is a cost accounting method that some companies and software utilize to calculate the cost of each activity in the manufacturing process. It identifies the cost drivers for each activity and provides a detailed breakdown of the costs. By analyzing this data, business owners can find inefficient activities and modify them.

Identify Profit Margins

Using software to calculate costs helps businesses determine the profit margin for each product or service. This data helps to identify inefficient products or services that may be underpriced or overpriced. Businesses can then enhance the profitability of their best products, services, and operations.

Using software can identify key areas that require more attention to costs and management. Businesses can develop strategies to mitigate unnecessary costs by examining these areas in detail. This leads to better cost control, resulting in improved profitability.

The Goals of Cutting Costs

The main goal is to eliminate unnecessary "bad" costs that can be used for "good" spending that boosts efficiency. Cost cutting specifically aims to:

1. Streamline and improve purchasing across the organization when different departments or teams need the same resources.

2. Reduce waste by cutting off spending on products, vendors, or processes that are not "worth it." To optimize the supply chain, you might stop paying for subscription services you are not using.

3. Reduce the chance of product returns from dissatisfied customers by enhancing quality assurance procedures.

4. Replace expensive acquisitions with cheaper alternatives if customer demand requires lower prices.

5. Outsource certain tasks to freelancers. For example, accounting tasks could be assigned to a specialized accounting firm that can do the job more effectively.

6. Repurpose existing tools and services in new ways to avoid the need for more acquisitions.

7. Optimize your workflows to reduce duplication, increase output, and lower operational costs.

8. Use technology to track business operations and look for opportunities to cut costs.

Why Is Cutting Costs Such a Crucial Process?

Cutting costs is hard, and careless execution can ruin a great effort. Accidentally cutting vital expenditures can lower the quality of your products, make the work harder for your employees, endanger your operations, and ultimately reduce your profit.

It is, therefore, not surprising that two out of every five businesses fail. Within the organization, cost reduction must be a formal, well-planned strategy that emphasizes long-term sustainability and has upper management and internal stakeholders' backing. Changing spending policies "on the spot" rarely produces the desired outcomes.

Every company's strategic approach to cost reduction is unique, as each has its spending habits, preferences, and market conditions. These factors affect how cost reduction operates within an organization.

Cost reduction requires considerable thought, but the benefits of success are evident. You get more out of your budget and can compete in your industry more effectively.

Cost Reduction Strategy

This is why it is pertinent that a business sets out cost-cutting guidelines and formulates strategies for different scenarios. While cost-cutting is effective, it should not be followed blindly, and costs should be carefully studied before any step is taken. This is why each strategy can be assigned to a cost type — best, good, and bad.

Let us start with the good things first. The best costs are those that allow an organization to grow its business and align with its customers. Customers' needs will depend upon the fulfillment of such costs as delivery and customer service. So, the best costs are those that should not be avoided because they allow a company to stand out from its competition and provide value for its customers.

The bad costs, in turn, are those that hamper the growth and end up being either a waste or a disutility for a business. The examples can include excessive marketing, research, and development costs for a medium-sized and established firm. Such funds can be used elsewhere to create or improve productivity.

Good costs are like great ones, although they can be managed over a period to maximize utility and productivity. A simple example of such a cost can be discounts and other benefits that are provided to customers throughout the year. During a time of financial trouble or economic uncertainty, a company may start to promote discounts to encourage early payments or increase orders/sales.

The classification of costs into types is important for this reason. It will allow you, as an entrepreneur or manager, to look out for bad costs and try to maximize the best costs in the hopes of sustainably growing your business. Also, we have mentioned and talked about cost-cutting, but it can also be through optimization that reduces costs and improves productivity — through the adoption of technology, monitoring, consulting, etc.

Beware when cutting costs or focusing on optimization since it can allow you to overcut costs that might appear unreal and hamper your organization's growth in the medium-to-long run.

"Setting the bar too high can look good on paper but it is likely that not only will you fail to achieve overambitious targets, you will also underfund the things your organization needs to grow," said Mr. Bant.[42]

Gartner conducted a study on businesses that has highlighted certain pressures on businesses post-COVID. This has led to the identification of some common mistakes that leaders make during cost-cutting in a turbulent time. The issue with hasty and uninformed strategies is that they are almost half as likely to not work in reducing costs.[43]

---

[42] Ibid.

[43] STAMFORD Conn, Gartner Says Finance Leaders Who Avoid Four Cost Management Mistakes Will Help Their Organizations Emerge Stronger From the COVID-19 Crisis, Gartner. October 26, 2020.
https://www.gartner.com/en/newsroom/press-releases/2020-10-26-gartner-says-finance-leaders-who-avoid-four-cost-

Things to Be Aware Of:

Do Not Aim for Unrealistic and Sporadic Cuts

As per the Gartner study, cuts can seem unachievable or counterproductive since they can hit where it matters the most — resources. The workforce, especially sales, works in tandem to create value for your products and allow you to remain in profit. If you focus directly on cutting salaries and wages, since they usually form a sizable chunk of expenses, then laying off people as the first measure might backfire.

You might lay off productive people or those who have huge chances of moving forward. Talent with crucial business information or important clients might be taken away by the laid-off worker. Another aspect of firing workers that is often ignored is in terms of compensation, severance, and benefits that a leaving employee is entitled to.

Furthermore, an unjustified firing in haste can result in legal costs and a fall in the workforce's morale. The costs associated with training staff are also quite high, and these are hidden costs that are good for the business if you retain the employees. Lastly, the shortage of labor and improving work

---

management-mistakes-will-help-their-organizations-emerge-stronger-from-the-covid19-crisis

culture following layoffs can be problematic for a small enterprise.

All these things must be considered when deciding to fire employees as a cost-reductive measure. A deeper understanding is what will lead to informed and effective strategies.

Sustain Change

Cost savings are effective if they increase productivity and are feasible in the long run without compromising the quality of work. Gartner has revealed that around eleven percent of businesses are able to sustain cost cuts for three years![44] This means that most companies do not have a strategy to sustain optimization in the long run.

Instead of focusing on a short-term benefit, try to think in the long-term and try to think about a cumulative benefit or loss as a measure of efficiency and decision-making. This will lead to consistency and stability in the business. When things are to be grown, it is the policies and processes that are often ignored.

Companies should instead focus on making work less complex to incentivize clarity and benefit in decision-making. This makes sense because the

---

[44] Ibid.

Gartner statement added that approximately six percent of businesses struggle due to a complex business structure. So, fewer products but better ones will lead to an increase in efficiency.

Fearing Innovation

The advent of digitalization of business has meant that small businesses fear an embracement of innovation and technology. It is noted that less than ten percent of companies utilize modern methods to grow.[45] Remaining traditional may help in running a large business if the revenue and profits are too big to sacrifice, but a gradual shift is the way to go.

Focusing on scaling in technology adoption and production is the sustainable and long-term approach that will lead you to win over future competition. This will also mean that your employees will be efficient over time and provide you with a much-needed beginner's advantage — especially if you are a small business in need of a boost.

"Companies that pulled ahead out of 2008 paid more attention to where their customer was going and protected costs that drove new growth. We know we can't cut our way to long-term sustainable growth. This recovery is an opportunity for leaders to

---

[45] Ibid.

rapidly go digital in everything they do. Meet customers in new ways, conduct work in new ways, and automate operations."[46]

In an uncertain economy, when every penny counts, even the smallest increase in revenue or cost-cutting can impact a company's profitability. The good news is a large-scale company overhaul is not necessary. It is often simple, common-sense steps within a cost-reduction strategy that improve the bottom line, especially for small businesses.

The end of the year is an excellent time to step back and look carefully at your business practices, but any time of the year will suffice. Take some time to consider what you are doing well and where you can improve before you implement cost-cutting measures for business.

Cost-advantage and Competition

Inflation can take a hit on your product or service. You should try to consider the factors before making any decisions to cut costs. Certainly, the uncomplicated way is an intended fall in quality, though this should never be thought of as an option. Instead, try to evaluate the value chain of your

---

[46] Fujifilm Business Innovation, 15 Cost-Cutting Ideas & Spend Optimization Tips for Your SME, Fujifilm website. n.d.
https://www.fujifilm.com/fbhk/en/insights/article/15-spend-optimization-tips-for-your-sme

product and industry and try to initiate savings on value. This means that negotiation with suppliers and the workforce will be crucial if you want to keep your costs competitive.

Major decisions, such as initiating work from home to save on rent or a smaller office, should be thoroughly evaluated and assessed against the benefits and requirements of your business.

The best thing to do is to first assess your costs against those of your competition. See where you can save and where you might have 'bad' costs that are holding your business down. If nothing seems to work, then try to find additional investment to improve your organization and its value chain. Lastly, inflation and uncertainty are part of living in an unpredictable world, but what you require is a realistic assessment.

If the costs become uncontrollable and unrealistic, then you may consider transferring the costs to the consumer. It is a realistic thing to do in such a case, though you should not be greedy about your profits in the short run. The point, at the end of the day, is to satisfy clients and retain them in the long run.

Growth that is not inclusive of your workforce or customers will not be sustainable; this strategy can also work when demand is weak and you want to improve your market share.[47] Such an approach can be useful for small companies or startups since their operational costs are low, and they can improve their market share and sales.

Conclusion

The right strategy will keep your business competitive. The methods streamline operational efficiency so that organizations get the most out of their employees and investments. The proper oversight of day-to-day expenses can transform struggling new businesses into profitable ones.

Cost reduction strategies can also free up opportunities for strategic resource allocation. They force companies to reassess their assets and focus on areas with a strong return on investment. That may mean allocating more resources to office equipment, the supply chain, digital resources, or raw materials.

Cost reduction is more than an antidote to unprecedented expenses. It can eliminate waste, too. Optimizing business expenses means a company invests in fewer low-value assets.

---

[47] Ibid.

Chapter 18: Cost Saving

We discussed the importance of cost-cutting in the last chapter and discussed what a strategy might feel like once you set it out. It will allow for productivity and profitability to improve, resulting in increased dividends for shareholders and satisfaction for the stakeholders. Cost reduction, leading to saving, in the long run, can allow a business to save enough funds to reinvest in development or expansion.

It can be difficult to ascertain whether lowering costs or increasing revenue is the silver bullet for cost saving. What can be said is there are a lot of factors that need to be considered when taking up cost-saving methods. Factors such as the nature of a business, its market, and economic conditions can all influence how costs can be saved.

At times when nothing can be understood or ascertained, focusing on marketing activities can be the key to financial stability and steadily increasing profits.

Extension of Cost-cutting

This chapter will focus on the actual ways of cost-saving, in practicality, and how all of this can help a business reduce its bad expenses and improve profitability in the long run.

The cost-cutting that your business adopts and how it extends can vary from industry to industry. Your goal — to increase cost-efficiency — can be to either cut costs or improve revenue, and your business's size can also play a role in how you strategize. Your profit margins need to be considered, too, since they are dependent on both net income and expenses.

Cost-cutting might not necessarily lead to increased profits. This is why there is a need to understand how to enact cost-saving in a structured manner to provide increased dividends in the long run. If anything, if done improperly, cost-cutting can lead to reduced revenues and dropped profits. You will need to concentrate on your branding and quality, set higher prices when required, and encourage a sustainable stream of sales that will lead to consistently increasing profit margins in the long run.

Reducing Costs and Profitability

The cost-cutting that your business adopts and how it extends can vary from industry to industry. Your goal — to increase cost-efficiency — can be to either cut costs or improve revenue, and your business's size can also play a role in how you strategize. Your profit margins need to be considered, too, since they are dependent on both net income and expenses.

Cost-cutting might not necessarily lead to increased profits. This is why there is a need to understand how to enact cost-saving in a structured manner to provide increased dividends in the long run. If anything, if done improperly, cost-cutting can lead to reduced revenues and dropped profits. You will need to concentrate on your branding and quality, set higher prices when required, and encourage a sustainable stream of sales that will lead to consistently increasing profit margins.

Reducing costs increases profitability, but only if sales prices and number of sales remain constant. If cost reductions result in a lowering of the quality of the company's products, then the company may be forced to reduce prices to maintain the same level of sales. This can wipe out any potential gains and result in a net loss.[48]

Improving Revenue

Cost saving and reduction usually aim to increase revenue to improve the profitability of a business.

---

[48] J.B. Maverick, Is It More Important for a Company to Lower Costs or Increase Revenue?, Investopedia.com. February 20, 2023.
Is It More Important for a Company to Lower Costs or Increase Revenue? (investopedia.com)

While your net profit margin may not necessarily increase, it will provide room for efficiency and growth in the short to medium term. But how good is a cost-saving measure if you increase costs elsewhere and fail to improve your profit margin?

Consider that you increase revenue by cutting costs, but this prop was due to hiring more people, and your profit margin did not increase at all. This usually happens when companies increase their workforce by a considerable number, either due to a new unit/product or double down on salespersons. This is a common issue that companies face, no matter how small or large they may be.

Let us take an example where a company doubles its revenue by increasing its sales from one to over two million dollars. If the increase was attributable to an increase in the workforce, say twice, from five to fifteen people with an average salary of one hundred thousand each. The additional revenue will then only result in a mere two hundred thousand, down from twenty percent to ten percent, if this increase was due to the hiring of more efficient staff of two rather than five average and similarly capable people.[49]

So, rather than focusing solely on increasing revenue, you can consider employing some additional

---

[49] Ibid.

workforce or experienced employees to increase your revenue efficiently and sustainably. In such cases, the company needs to be clear about its goals, as with any other strategy.

Every organization needs to ensure whether they want a lower profit margin in the short-run for a long-term gain or an absolute improvement in profits for short-to-medium-term goals. For instance, a company might focus on a short-term increase in profitability to secure a loan or investment. Similarly, an increase in revenue can be a push to secure funds for expansion and improve cash flow.

It is important to understand that an increase in revenue and profits is not necessarily a reflection of improved cash flows. Sales, for instance, may be on credit and on softer terms that may end up hurting your working capital. Similarly, a lowering of expenses and an increase in revenue is not necessarily evidence of a healthy or financially secure business.

Cost Saving These Days

With businesses these days, the strategy is to do more with less and look for the best and most efficient tools and methods to save on costs. It is the Holy Grail for new start-ups and tech businesses alike. From savings costs on small offices or shared co-working spaces to adopting efficient and paperless strategies, a lot of time and resources get saved on everyday tasks.

Menial tasks such as printing and emailing have increasingly been taken over by *Microsoft Excel, Slack, Dropbox,* and *WhatsApp.* This means that there are fewer steps involved in tasks, and it is more than easy to access data and conduct analysis than before. So, the savings in paper, printing, and mailing costs have also increased productivity.

This means that there is more time for businesses to concentrate on their products and services. The quality of products and delivery of services can now be easily maintained and even improved over time. There are many ways that costs can be saved, for instance, via automation, centralized systems, and modern software/tools.

Say Goodbye to The Manual Work

Software and platforms are used by businesses to cut down on costs or improve productivity. There are different industry standards for such technologies. However, the need to implement any type of strategy adopted will depend solely on the nature of the business (product, service, and manufacturing) and its scale of operations (small, medium, and large).

Automation

If a business wants to save costs and increase productivity and profitability, then consider automating certain services and processes. For example, the time spent on manually entering data from physical sheets can be assisted using scanner applications on handheld devices to be recognized by AI and exported into the file format of your choice — from PDF, word, excel, or database documents.

Similarly, analytical tasks on spreadsheets that used to be tedious and time-consuming can now be quickly done through powerful business systems and applications. Imagine using a service to automate data processing to save valuable time and gain quick insights. This would mean that resources are available for customer service and service delivery. Management will also improve as a result, and the time saved can be utilized for improving the business's performance.

Datarails is an example of a system to automate, collectivize and visualize data reporting from different platforms – such as Excel, etc., without the use of coding or additional software — and markets that the system can help save up to half a million dollars, ninety-hours of reporting/analysis time, and improve productivity by almost fifty percent![50]

In addition, the reconciliation of statements, analysis of datasets, and paperwork management can all be handled using modern platforms and cloud-based services that improve availability and accessibility. This is important when we are evaluating business performance and improving turnover time for processes and tasks. For instance, financial software for payroll can help make the lives of HR easier, providing them valuable time for other essential tasks such as improving training, morale, and productivity of the workforce.

Similarly, with the advent of AI and cloud-based tools, tax filing has also been made efficient and simple. Intuit's software across North America, Australia, Europe, and England means that people with little to no understanding of tax laws can file their taxes efficiently and not have to worry about tax codes. This saves essential money for small businesses and startups since they cannot afford expensive accountants, lawyers, and tax consultants.

---

[50] The product is not endorsed, but provided as an example to aid the readers and make them understand how productivity is being improved and cost is being cut these days. The software is an example of automation with Microsoft Excel and it can help a lot in the business functions of marketing, sales, finance and human resources.
Source: DataRails website — https://www.datarails.com/

Financial reporting has also been made easier in a comparable manner, and accounting software can provide increased value to businesses. With timely execution and oversight of payments and finances, businesses can make decisions more quickly and effectively than ever before. This will also allow you to reduce staff and help them concentrate on improving their productivity elsewhere.

The most of automation these days is that it can lead to the centralization of processes and systems to be implemented later in various departments of an organization. All this means that profitability will surely increase, with much room for growth since resources will be freed up to be reallocated toward customers. Service delivery will also improve as processes become streamlined and simplified.

It might not sound as easy as it is, but efficiency and streamlining of workflow are two important tasks that should continue throughout the company. They help reduce operational costs, improve the budget, and increase the well-being of employees since they can be relaxed under less pressure. Also, the costs associated with a lack of modern or extensive software mean that invoicing and file maintenance can be headaches and time-consuming.

Given that time is money, platforms that maintain master data for billing, receivables, and customer service are crucial in today's modern age. A survey recently found that under nine hundred of the worst-performing companies had to spend nine dollars on average to invoice a customer. In comparison, the best-performing companies spent two dollars on each invoice, and the median value was just shy of four dollars.

Accounting software can help reduce costs and recognize timely payments. Business growth would eventually mean an increase in invoices and sales and a decrease in errors. This can help build lasting relationships with customers.

Centralized Systems

A company with a centralized record system is something that can help any organization in any department. This makes a business well suited to hitting the required targets and margins to improve the sales line.

In some cases, such as that of Excel, it is also problematic for some software. This is because the analysis is manual, and preparation for reports requires the assistance of professionals such as those for audit, cost, and professional accounting. They will require at least thirty hours per month, according to fifteen thousand dollars per month — just for reporting.[51]

In such cases, centralized systems and specialized software can work in tandem to generate modern, cloud-based, and automated solutions. This will free up resources that can be used elsewhere, making the company more profitable than before and increasing the productivity of the employees. This will mean that the time utilization for important tasks can be concentrated, and the additional workload can be managed by your team.

The benefits of automation tend to add up over time, and they will help your company succeed in the medium-to-long run. So, how else can businesses save their money, especially by avoiding simple or free software?

Consider the case of TransAlta, which ended up having millions of dollars in losses due to a literal 'cut-and-paste' error in Microsoft Excel that caused transmission contracts to be bought multiple times over. Similarly, companies have lost important equity and value due to overestimation and incorrect data insights from regular spreadsheet errors. So, the sole reliance on Excel for data reporting should be avoided if the revenue has increased by over a million dollars.

---

[51] Ibid.

In accounting and finance, it is important not to lose unnecessary money and instead to run and manage reports periodically. Your work should be of a prominent level. It will save hours, and your employees can help with hours elsewhere. Also, modern software pays them for themselves in less time and provides confidence through useful insights.

Cost-saving Systems

How do you begin to assess if your business is ready for such a huge technological investment or not? It is simple. Follow suit and think about the value overall. Consider the monthly and yearly costs that each system would replace or eventually save.

You can narrow down the saved costs by departments and budget accordingly to determine where the benefit would be most utilized. Start in this manner and use inventory and furniture that is used to save money. At the same time, try to evaluate your subscriptions and set realistic expectations.

Once you begin to trim down your operations, your business will become much more efficient than before. Do not concentrate on rushing to increase revenue because a sustainable method will require some time for results to flourish.

Eventually, you will realize and witness the results. You will be able to figure out what areas require your focus and attention. Also, the efficient units and departments will become prominent so you can concentrate on them and allocate resources appropriately.

Once your systems are in place, then you can slowly begin to adopt technology overall in your business. You will be able to accomplish company-wide efficiency and streamline workflow processes. This will help with the integration of technology in your company and increase efficiency many times over eventually.

You can improve productivity by over ninety percent since a lot of your time and money would have been saved.[52] This is what would drive the productivity of your business.

Feel-good Savings

So, when you have implemented systems, you will be able to understand your numbers better and implement informed and realistic goals. The cost reduction will be driven through technology and a standardized system. This will ensure that your

---

[52] Ibid.

employees are happier and more productive than before.

You will be able to compete well and survive in an agile and productive manner. Your decisions and goals will be intelligent, and simple tasks will become automated. Analytics will drive your insights and simplify tasks.

The time and money saved on reducing the tac-time for tasks and errors in reporting will mean a difference in your long-term growth. Businesses that spend less time on repetitive tasks can get more things done and create more value than ever. The power of AI and cloud-based platforms also means that your reports will be generated quickly and easily.

Your reports will be shared and accessible to those who matter in any format possible. Some platforms also provide the service of a real-time dashboard — leading to rounded and advanced insights.

The Six Types of Cost Savings

So, cost-saving is freeing up your money through a change in policy and plan that minimizes the costs of operations. It is a strategy that deploys a more outward and long-term approach to supply consistent and sustainable gains. The resultant output will improve profitability and the financial health of a company.

Six types of cost savings are commonly used — from budget to index-based to technical. They can be used to lower your costs and are as follows:

Historic Savings

These savings are based on the change compared to the previous period. It is a method to calculate your costs, year-on-year, and help establish a baseline. For instance, you might utilize a historical comparison to see how much your product's price or costs have increased to assess profitability and changes in condition.

Budget Savings

This form of saving is based on the concept of your price compared to your budgeted costs. You derive the difference between the final costs and the budgeted costs to ascertain cost savings.

Technical Savings

This method can be attributed to a change in the specification or dimensions of a product. Your cost-savings may be derived due to a change in material or weight of it. For example, if rapid price changes in a component require you to switch from silver to copper, then the resultant difference in budgeted prices will lead you to save through the material costs or technical specifications.

Request for Proposal (RFP) Savings

RFP savings entail a saving that results from the initially quoted costs to those received for an actual product. This can be a quite helpful strategy, especially when placing RFPs from multiple vendors to receive the best price. The savings resulting from this process will allow you to select the lowest bidder and receive efficiency in costs.

Index Savings

This is a method that utilizes an index to mark the development and trend of the costs. You might try to procure or produce a product that is five percent cheaper than the index for your product to become competitive. Similarly, your product might be heavier and stronger in density to be more durable than the competition.

Ratio Savings

This saving method is a combination of savings. For example, you may combine the benefits of indexed and RFP-based savings to determine the contribution that each method provided to your savings.

Both the employees and the employer have a role in cost-saving. For the employer, it is his responsibility to ensure that policies are in place to ensure cost-saving measures are implemented. The employee, on the other hand, has the sole responsibility of ensuring he/she adheres to the stipulated measures.

Summing Up Cost Saving

So, how will we keep up with using cost-saving strategies and finding areas you might need to concentrate on? It is simple. You can follow the simple advice pointers to be strategic about your cost savings.

Substitution

The simplest way to save on costs is to substitute them. If there is a cheaper alternative out there of a standard that is comparable to your current/required one, then adopt it. This allows your product or service to become competitive and lets you avoid unnecessary cost cuts that may be good and affect productivity. For instance, when using licenses for productivity tools, you can utilize open-source products that are free and competitive. This will help create a lot of room for savings and productivity without sacrificing productivity.

A lot of research must be conducted to find substitutes, and they should be adopted once there is a clear winner. Your competitiveness will mean the difference between your company's profitability and survivability in the long run.

Combination

This is a method that requires you to utilize a common cost between two or more business functions. This will reduce your costs for each unit and make them efficient. This will also improve your profitability eventually if you find a cheaper alternative to the cost. For instance, you may consider finding a common vendor for a common service, such as upkeep at two business units, to gain a discount or better price.

This will provide you with a better choice and service. It is also a method to keep the costs low in the short-to-medium run.

Adaptation

At times, simple strategies do not work because the problem is not internal but rather external. In such a case, you can try to adapt to a changing situation and analyze how the competitors or your industry has reacted before. This will allow you to embrace the situation and improvise accordingly.

For example, what would you do if you realized that the insurance costs are going high because of interest rates, and this is going to increase your cost of borrowing too? You may want to reduce your assets or lease some of them to reduce the burden. Similarly, rising costs of production might want you to consider 'shrinking' your products to maintain competitiveness and overall price in an economically turbulent time.

At the same time, you also want to consider changing your preferred choice of employment — by switching from full-time to part-time employees and consultants. This can allow you to save on required costs such as benefits, contributions, and rewards.

Modification

When faced with an inconvenient situation like adaptation, you may want to reconsider how you approach a certain cost. What would you do if suddenly people began to provide more incentives to employees in your industry?

You may have to consider permanently improving pay and benefits to incentivize workers. While this may allow you to increase costs in the short term, it would allow you to avoid the hefty cost of severance packages that would have to be provided in case of redundancies. The situation would require that you show loyalty to your employees, so you would have to modify your operations.

At the same time, you may consider moving your employees remotely to save on other benefits and costs that you would otherwise have to appropriate at the office.

Reallocation

Reallocating resources can also reduce your business costs. You might need to find different utilities for a cost or suggest ways they may amalgamate with other business units. For instance, you may want to consider appropriating a common kitchen for your staff instead of having one for executives and one for other employees.

Similarly, you may want to reconsider buying used or refurbished furniture for your office and a smaller office in an extreme situation. This will allow you to avoid investing in modern furniture and reduce costs without compromising on the utility of the fixtures.

Elimination

Finally, do not cut costs until they need to be and there is no other alternative. To begin with, it can be expensive to find replacements often and problematic in some cases. The case of making a position redundant or firing an employee can be costly.

The costs associated with redundancies can be huge since a lot of legal obligations make it costly. Instead of having to pay a severance package or having to pay for a lawsuit in the case, you can instead try to reassign positions or reduce work hours. If you want to save further on costs, then you can provide an option for remote work at lower pay.

The need to be cautious about cost elimination is important. Instead, costs should be rationalized and thought of with a long-term perspective. You may fire an employee during a challenging time, but it may be next to impossible to rehire that hard-working person after a year or two.

This is why there is a serious need to understand and ponder upon costs and their types. The bad, good, and great costs come together to play a huge role in how cost-saving can be conducted. When nothing else works, try to review costs and evaluate them against their value and productivity.

You also need to embrace technology whenever possible to adapt to a changing world and improve your business's efficiency. This will allow you to stick to a budget and concentrate on important things.

Whenever possible, try to find alternatives to expensive goods and services and keep your marketing costs low/manageable. If there is a cheap or free avenue to advertise, then utilize it and do it sustainably in the long run. Finally, keep your customers and employees happy!

A fit and efficient team will always bring in more leads and revenue. At the same time, you would not have to worry about their motivation or having to push them to bring results. Your customers will be the happiest in the end.

At the end of the day, if you follow these steps, then you will have saved costs and avoided blunders and common mistakes. This is why you must make your experience count and think of cost saving in the long rather than the short run.

If you still need help, then you can feel free to join associations within your industry to gain insights and find avenues of support. You will receive exclusive discounts and access to resources and information that will prove invaluable. Also, when possible and stuck, do not waste time making uninformed decisions and seek professional help to act swiftly and aptly!

Chapter 19: CFO Services

Once you have optimized your business plan and laid out strategies accordingly, your organization will begin to witness growth that is regularly coordinated and flowing. As your revenues start to grow over the years, your need to structure your financial planning will be the key to your success. You will need to keep track of your cash flow and review and develop sustainable growth strategies.

All this will be based on the financial condition of your organization and define your future successes. This means that these responsibilities will fall on your shoulders as an entrepreneur or manager, and you will either need to serve the role of or hire a Chief Financial Officer (CFO).

A CFO is a key financial officer in any business, and its primary role is to oversee and ensure the smooth functioning of the financial operation of an organization. This means making important decisions that can increase financial strengths and avoid any shortcomings — depending on the business's financial standing.

Virtual CFO

Since hiring a CFO is a lengthy and expensive endeavor, I would not recommend it for startups and new or restructured organizations. The high, often seven-figure salaries and rewards of a reputable CFO are worth it for organizations that are established and have a financial workforce that can reap the benefits of such a talent. This can be a useful strategy once your business becomes established and requires expansion and growth.

Until such stability and success can be achieved, the CFO services can be outsourced and remotely managed by consultancies and third-party experts. This is a viable alternative since it is scalable, cost-effective, and productive. You virtually gain the same services as that of a CFO.

The best part is that your preferred level of expertise and valuable insights into a company's finances can be provided by a virtual CFO at your disposal. You will also save on office space, bonuses, and other costs that a full-time CFO would otherwise require to function well.

Benefits

The most obvious benefit of a virtual CFO is certainly the cost-saving, but it will help your organization in many other ways and prove to be quite more effective than a full-time CFO. The best part is that these virtual services are affordable and competitive. The price advantage is that they are according to your needs, and you only pay for what you require.

Flexibility

So, depending on your deliverables, reports, and requirements, you can check and ascertain how much expenses you will need to set out each time you avail of the virtual CFO services. It will help you save crucial time and resources on other product development, production, research, and, most importantly, marketing and sales!

Similarly, you can also scale the hours that you require to work or just order services for a fixed period. You will also be able to adapt as your business's needs evolve, and you will save your business from expensive consultant costs. This will pave the way for you to integrate technology and plan your business.

Technology and Budgeting

Your remote CFO service providers will also be efficient in providing you with feedback and analysis. This is often because you will be able to hire an expert team that can quickly process your financial data and turn it into actionable insight. At the same time, your business's efficiency increases because you will be able to project the requirements of your business in the short to medium run.

Your business's financial projections and actual numbers can be compared to help you re-evaluate how your next budget might look. This will enable you to identify key areas that need to be focused on and worked upon. It will allow for a meaningful and sustainable strategy for growth.

At the same time, with improved efficiency and advanced analytics, your cash flow will significantly improve in no time. You will also be able to act on the insights provided once you save money and improve your cash flow! Your business's spending patterns will become evident and allow you to enact workable and efficient solutions to improve business efficiency and cash flow.

Diversity and Experience

The most distinct benefit that a virtual CFO will provide you with will be to take advantage of working with a high-level professional(s) and be able to collaborate with cross-industry experiences. This is invaluable for new or struggling businesses since they can gain knowledge and insights from other industries through virtual experts. At the same time, it will improve your business's project management and collaboration capabilities.

An expert who is detached from your business will also be able to provide you with insights that are unbiased and well-informed. A full-time CFO might overlook certain factors due to work pressure or lack of exposure, and your business might suffer as a result.

An added advantage of a virtual CFO is that it will also prepare you and your business for a stage when you will eventually have a full-time CFO and be able to reap the full benefits from it. The diverse industry experience gained from virtual CFOs will mean that you will be able to set the room for future growth and completely utilize the skillsets being offered by a full-time CFO in the future. Since CFOs are experts in accounting, finance, and economics, you will also be able to gain access to their contacts and network.

Such a network will be beneficial when you expand into new products, services, and regions. A diverse and dedicated CFO service will also allow you to handle challenges constructively. This can also be a learning opportunity for you and your staff to understand and train in strategy.

Access to a diverse experience will allow your organization to learn how to handle financial needs without spending a fortune on a full-time CFO. The various stages of growth and challenges will be dealt with quickly by virtual CFOs. The ability of your organization to deal with technology and implement digital transformation can also improve as virtual technology is utilized for communicating and working with a virtual CFO.

This opportunity will provide your business with the ability to respond to ever-changing situations. The confidence that will come through a virtual CFO will also equip your organization to make decisions based on actionable insights and real-time data. This is an essential value that every new business or start-up needs to build.

Virtual CFO as a Financial Strategy

Startups and technology-focused businesses are increasingly open to virtual CFOs as a financial strategy to save on costs and grow sustainably. The ability to outsource CFO services means that your organization is not dependent on one person, but rather can gain from the experience of many in a short period. The risks are divided, and fiscal management becomes improved as a result.

The greatest benefit a virtual CFO will provide is activating and incentivizing your bookkeeping staff. He will keep the team on its toes and remain up to date on any tax or compliance issues before they arise. Your new team will gain a lot from an experienced virtual CFO, and he will indirectly be able to motivate them.

This means that your accounting will be professional and maintained. You will also be able to generate reports and analyses quickly and push your business to the next level using accurate data. Also, your organization will save valuable training time and resources that would alternatively be required to spend on your team otherwise.

Another benefit of a virtual CFO, as a financial strategy, can be for a struggling business. Oversight of an expert and the frank opinion of an outsider might just allow you to witness any shortcomings that may have been missed and find solutions that are reliable and effective. A single person leading a new organization can also be a challenge for a full-time CFO and might lead to wrong decisions that dearly cost your business.

Remote financial officers can also help curtail the pressure that a new business owner might feel to serve the role of a CFO. This decision can be damaging for your business if you do not have a commercial and financial understanding of your business.

Reporting and Accountability

Accurate reporting will flow from a professional officer's supervision in your new organization and can allow you to know the frank and true situation of your business. Complete information will mean your decisions are informed, and you will be able to track the organization's financial situation. This will ensure that your budgeting, planning, and reporting are all aligned and future oriented.

This will ensure that your business has accountability for every business transaction. Every decision-maker will be able to work professionally and contribute to their duties. Your bookkeeper may have initially managed your accounting, too; however, it will become possible to separate the duties between the two as your business grows.

Your assets will also be controlled by a professional to present accurate data to the management and allow them to make and inform accurate data. You will be able to focus on achieving your objectives.

A Well-informed Management

Since you may have started a business out of your love for something other than crunching numbers, your management must be informed every minute. This will ensure that your strategy is not an arrow in the air but rather a responsible and serious gesture. Your management will be able to understand what worked versus what did not work.

Once you know how well your organization may be financially performing, you gain confidence to adapt and refine your strategies accordingly. You will also be able to raise capital if your organization has a robust financial system in place and accurate information.

Bankers, lenders, and investors are always interested in having clear and reliable information that is backed by accurate data. If you do so, then you will be able to ascertain the growth and related strategies to raise capital too. Your virtual CFO will be able to provide you with a strategy to explain what failed and what can succeed.

This will also help you avoid a catastrophe in your business and provide an opportunity to achieve your business and growth goals. You will be able to do so economically and sustainably. So, what reporting and budgeting will you be able to do once you let this strategy be adopted?

Reporting and Budget

Once your virtual CFO service is set up and running, you will be able to design reports that are tailored and effective at providing the relevant information to you. It will enable an opportunity for you to understand where your business currently stands and where it is headed. Maintained and standardized reporting will allow your CFO service to take less time to maintain your records.

The time saved can be used by your staff to ensure compliance and maintain checks and balances to strengthen your organization's reporting. The virtual CFO service can also suggest and maintain the appropriate and latest financial software to suit your business's needs. Like your business's accounting, your IT department will also benefit from this strategy and learn to implement the relevant software.

Once your business's reporting is streamlined, it will set a path for your business to generate an appropriate and realistic budget based on accurate financial information. This can set the difference between your company achieving its plans and making balanced business decisions. It can also help you find the right investment and avoid making a crucial mistake.

As a Guide to Success

Some CFO services can also prepare you for board meetings and convince investors to receive the true picture of your business. As an entrepreneur or manager, you may require strategic guidance to handle management matters and execute decisions that are best for your business. Coaching is the element that might allow you to rally your stakeholders and see your vision.

The difference between a couple of successful investment and idea pitches is what startups and struggling businesses require to change their direction toward success. You can accurately and effectively present the information required and reveal your plans to your investors.

Types of CFO Services

Given the benefits of virtual CFOs, it is equally important to understand that there is a variety of services that you can avail yourself of these days. You should explore the following avenues of growth and improvement to turn your business into a success:

- **Virtual CFOs :** The most common and already discussed throughout the chapter. These are usually agencies that offer long-term services to your financial management needs. They typically lend dedicated staff to help and manage your financial unit, but they are not location-based or involved in the day-to-day operations of your company.

- **Consultants:** These are the most common service providers who can work on a contractual basis. They work from project to project and help execute a variety of management and strategic projects — from fulfilling procedures to setting up technology. These teams involve highly experienced professionals, including CFOs, who can provide mentoring and clarity to your business units.

They usually work short-to-medium terms to set up important projects and tasks for companies. They aim to help businesses improve their strategy, decision-making, and reporting. This is why some of them can also serve as interim CFOs on certain projects or while your organization passes through a transition phase.

- **Single Source CFOs:** This is a one-person operation that provides CFO services for multiple clients. You would want to make sure this individual is familiar with your specific industry and can meet your needs if you (or another client) have an urgent, all-in project.

- **Third-party Agencies**: These agencies provide specialized staff who can help with your industry and provide expert advice. They are not limited to providing virtual CFOs, but they can provide you with technical staff of all kinds. They excel at finding those who may be the best fit for your industry.

- **CFO Consortiums:** These are professional organizations that aim to provide consulting services to organizations in a certain geographic region or industry. They are useful when businesses want to execute strategic and technical projects in the medium to long run but do not possess the expertise or resources to do so. They can help guide and provide services that enable such management decisions.

So, to sum up, various advantages are associated with a CFO service over employing a full-time CFO. Other than the monetary and strategic benefits highlighted above, the additional one is that such a service will provide professional and strategic insights and inputs before an organization is established. This helps businesses gain an outlook and vision to reform and report flawlessly before hiring a full-time CFO.

The other aspect that needs to be highlighted is that virtual CFOs can help expand the sophistication level and scope of a startup or struggling business. An established and successful CFO can help lay the ground for a structure and design that encourages growth and continuity in the long run.

Financial System and Design

Utilizing a remote CFO service online or using financial software alone will not allow you to reap the benefits and achieve growth. The best thing that you can do before or during the time you utilize the service of a virtual CFO is to find services that are incompatible or lacking in your business. This will provide you with an opportunity to truly grow and expand your organization's financial system.

It is an indirect approach since a remote CFO service will usually not be able to help implement an actual system but analyze and guide you for current and future needs. This will allow you to work out a roadmap for your organization's success in the short and long run. You will be able to execute strategies and a smart design as well as run a system smoothly and sustainably.

You will have ample time to train your workforce and prepare them for the changes in the structure. A well-designed financial system in your organization can mean the difference between how efficient your CFO or CFO services will be and ensure your success eventually.

Conclusion

Once your reporting is straightened, a virtual CFO's projections will sit well with your stakeholders and allow you and your managers to present the information appealingly. There will also be fewer chances of errors and gaps in data, resulting in optimum chances of gaining additional funding and investment. This will help you set realistic targets and goals to meet your organization's vision.

Improved financial reporting and design will lead your cash flow and financial strategy to be accurately analyzed and accordingly restructured (as required). Since cash flow is one of the most crucial elements of a business's survivability, you need to have accurate data to highlight and resolve issues before they become unmanageable or complicated.

Outsourced CFOs can allow your organization to identify essential expenses from non-essential ones. This will ensure that your organization's financial health improves and that you focus on what is important. Their experience is unrivaled, especially for struggling organizations and startups.

Your business's drive toward growth and profitability can be achieved through virtual CFOs and relevant services. They will provide unbiased and unrivaled guidance, which is not only strategic and effective but also budget-friendly.

The flexibility and affordability of virtual CFOs can also mean the difference for struggling and young organizations. Such a service will free up resources and allow you to focus on sales, innovation, and growth. Businesses can also navigate through tough times and impartially enact strategic decisions through virtual CFOs.

Step 5: Tax Reduction Plan

Chapter 20: Introduction

All of us want to file our taxes on time, and it is crucial for businesses to remember Tax Day — typically April 15th of each year, unless it falls on a holiday or weekend. Most of us treat taxes like a task at the job we hate but do it for the sake of it. There are a lot of benefits attached to it once you begin to understand the process and how it works.

To start with, anything that you do with consciousness and awareness will lead you to feel both happy and satisfied. In order to feel that when filing taxes, you need to have an understanding of tax rates, taxable income, rebates, reductions, and related tax codes. This can seem cumbersome to many, which is why they simply resort to using software such as TurboTax or Intuit to file taxes. However, you can save a lot of money if you have a working knowledge of taxes and if you do some planning beforehand.

Like businesses, individuals should also plan for the tax year ahead in advance and pay attention to their business income and taxes. The first thing to understand in order to achieve tax reduction is to know that it is legal to save your money from taxes if you know which category is applicable to each income or expense type.

Other than that, there are various federal, state, and local laws at play that need to be tapped to secure your income. Otherwise, you will just end up paying more on basic things such as social security, 401K, IRAs, and Medicare.

Tax Reduction

Taxes are difficult to avoid, but this does not mean that you should stop yourself from planning for taxes and income in advance. For instance, you can have a strategy in place to secure your investments through a tax-exempt trust fund to hold your securities and savings. You will eventually have to pay taxes, which is your duty as a law-abiding citizen, but you need to know that you can maximize your gains through knowledge of tax brackets and types.

So, let us try to understand taxable income and tax brackets before we delve into tax reduction strategies and tax planning. You have certain taxes that you owe to the federal, state, and local governments. For instance, the federal tax is applicable on the percentage of taxable income that you owe to the IRS.

You should know that tax brackets are applicable to you, and taxable income should not be confused with adjusted gross income (AGI). AGI is your gross income without the deductions applied that are to be deducted by the IRS.[53] On the other hand, taxable income is your adjusted gross income minus the allowances for personal exemptions and itemized deductions.

These deductions are also referred to as below-the-line deductions. So, once you know your taxable income, you can use the federal tax brackets from the IRS's website, software, or a tax consultant to determine your maximum tax. This is important because you will know how much of your income is taxable, so you may divide it into parts to ascertain which amount can be appropriated to a suitable category.

This is because business owners and high-income individuals should always know how each dollar they earn or spend is categorized —to know how it will be taxed. This opens the ground for tax deductions, which help reduce the tax liability of a taxpayer. This is done by lowering the AGI and, thereby, taxable income.

The more deductions you find, the lower your tax bill will be, and this will lead to a higher amount to save or invest. But how will you plan for taxes in

---

[53] Michelle P. Scott, 6 Strategies to Protect Income from Taxes, Investopedia.com. April 30, 2023.
https://www.investopedia.com/articles/personal-finance/032116/top-6-strategies-protect-your-income-taxes.asp

advance if you do not know about tax rules and strategies?

Small businesses often employ various tax reduction strategies to manage their tax liabilities and maximize their after-tax income. Some of the common tax-minimizing strategies are as follows:

- **Structure Selection:** The first and foremost thing that is considered when establishing a business is to identify the type of corporate structure under which the business is going to operate, as discussed above. The corporate structure of the business has a significant impact on its tax implications. Each structure has its own merits and demerits when it comes to managing taxation. It is essential to choose the structure that best fits the needs and objectives of the business.
- **Income and Expenses Scheduling:** Properly timing the income and expenses of the business can positively impact the taxable income. For instance, deferring the income to the following tax year and accelerating deductible expenses to the current year can help manage and shift the tax liability to a more favorable time.
- **Employing Family Members:** The perks of employing family members to your business could be the fact that their wages could be deducted from the business expense and, hence, the income could be shifted to lower tax brackets.
- **Section 179 Depreciation:** Small businesses could greatly benefit from Section 179 of the Internal Revenue Code (IRC), which allows for the cost deduction of certain qualifying properties, such as

equipment and machinery, etc., in the year it came in use rather than depreciating it over several years.

Tax Planning and Strategy

While we will explore tax planning in detail in the next chapter, through the strategy, knowing the basics can be the right place to begin with. Tax planning pertains to the analysis and arrangement of finances in a systematic manner. By categorizing and understanding expenses and income, one can maximize tax breaks and minimize tax liabilities in a legal and efficient manner.

Tax rules are often lengthy and can be complicated to understand for people. Taking some time out to know and use them for your benefit can entirely change how much you end up paying and receiving back returns when you file. One simple thing that consultants and businesses do is find appropriate expenses.

Taxable Income and Expenses

Given that the nature of expenses is contra-income, they are generally not directly eligible for taxes because they ultimately reduce your profits. You also can't plan for the future if you are unable to pinpoint your present situation and tax bracket(s). Given that the American tax system is progressive in nature, this means higher taxable incomes are subject to higher tax rates and vice versa.

This is why you should mention any expenses you made and purchase additional business items such as machinery, furniture, or stock to reduce your tax bill. At the same time, spending on assets will allow you to increase your capital and save yourself from inflation. You can also save yourself from having to spend the amount in the future when business may be uncertain and you may need more time to spare the cash.

You can use this understanding to plan for your expenses in advance or even do so properly to have appropriate tax deductions. This is why taxable income is not the same as total income. It helps explain why your taxable income is not simply multiplied by the tax bracket.

The government divides your taxable income into categories and then taxes each one as per the relevant rate. For instance, if you earn over thirty-two thousand, then you fall in the twelve percent tax slab. However, you do not pay so on the entire amount. You adjust for the basic rate on the minimum amount, then pay the percentage of your bracket on the remaining amount.

Tax Credits and Tax Deductions

This brings us to tax credits, which we all love, and this may be the best part about filing taxes. These are the tax returns, the amount you overpaid that you receive back, and so people always want to maximize them. This is often through certain expenses, which we incur, and they ultimately end up reducing our tax bill.

So, a tax credit of two thousand dollars will reduce your tax bill by two thousand. This leaves us with standard deductions. These are simple, no-brainer tax deductions. They make taxes simple, turn the tax process faster, and are a common technique that many businesses and people deploy.

This is why Congress sets the amount of the standard deduction, and it is typically adjusted every year for inflation. The standard deduction that you qualify for depends on your filing status. So, there is a limit to this technique, but there is another way to save more money and pay less taxes.

Itemize Expenses

This brings us to the itemization of expenses. It is an important part of our plan since knowing this can allow you to prioritize what needs to be treated as a standard deduction. This can mean a huge difference on your tax bill. Basically, you itemize deductions you or your business qualify for — one by one. This is done if the standard deduction range does not fulfill your expenses.

An added benefit is that we can plan our taxes throughout the year this way. The only difference is that it might take more time to do taxes since the items are increased. You also have to prove your qualification for deductions, which can be matched against the IRS's Schedule A to claim itemized deductions.

If used strategically, itemized deductions can protect your income and prove to be attractive. If you own a property, you apply deductions on it and also on the interest that you pay on the mortgage. This will allow you to save a large chunk of your money. Depending on the state, you can itemize property on your tax return, even if you have opted for standard deductions.

Protecting Your Income

If you are a business owner or an investor, you can contribute to your retirement and employee benefits account if you are employed by an organization. The best benefit is that some of your pretax income can become exempt income from taxation, and you will be able to defer income taxes on other earnings.

Similarly, if you invest on a long-term scheme, then the tax rates will be low on them, and you will certainly earn a lot more this way than investing in the short-term. At the same time, if you invest in stocks or incur a loss, a capital loss deduction will allow you to reduce taxes further when you need your money the most.

There are also many municipal bonds, which are generally not subject to federal tax. This is because you are lending money to a state or local government. Once the maturity is reached, the investment will be returned along with the interest.

In some cases, these bonds are also exempt from local and state laws. This is why tax-free interest payments make municipal bonds attractive to investors. While they have a lower rate of return, they are less likely to default and secure your investment.

The low return, combined with no tax, makes these bonds quite lucrative and investor-friendly. So, if you have a considerable amount that you earn, have saved, or want to invest and secure, buy a municipal bond from it to make your investment tax-free. The higher your income, the higher your tax savings will be.

Aim for the Long-term

Investing in stocks and other mutual funds is quite different, but investing over the long run will result in favorable tax treatment. This is given the nature of capital gains, which are taxed the most on the year an investment is made. So, if you hold an asset— fund, property, or stock and sell it within a year, then you have to pay a percentage on the gain, which is relatively high.

Selling year(s) later can result in rates between zero percent and twenty percent, depending on the state and the number of years an investment is held. For instance, the zero percent tax is applied on $44,625 for singles, whereas it is $89,250 for couples for the year. The applicable amounts have been increased by around three thousand for singles, compared to six thousand for couples.

You can analyze the pattern of increases over the years and compare it with inflation rates to determine and pan for future tax-free brackets. This is how efficient planning can help save people thousands of dollars every year. Similarly, losses can also be cited to gain tax credits.

This ensures that the tax liability on the sale of assets does not hit you twice during a loss. Losses in capital of less than three thousand can be adjusted in the same year's income tax returns. Anything over three thousand in loss can be carried over the future to adjust the tax bills efficiently.

Business and Benefits

If you create income from freelancing or consulting, then you can register your own business. Having a business offers a lot of tax advantages. For instance, if you own a business, a lot of the expenses can be deducted from your income, leading to a reduced total tax bill. Similarly, the benefits provided to employees — such as health insurance and social security contributions — have tax deductions when requirements are met.

These contributions can also be catered to business owners. In fact, self-employed persons can also benefit from them — leading to meeting insurance premiums, increasing 401K contributions, and ensuring reduced tax bills. You will also secure your health and future by maximizing the benefits.

Some of the home-owner expenses can be attributed to deductions under home-office deductions. For instance, internet and other utility bills can also be deducted from income, although the requirement is to have a profit on the business. Similarly, a business is considered to be profitable if it has profited in three of the last five years.

To incentivize employers to contribute to their employees' retirement benefits, Setting Every Community Up for Retirement Enhancement (SECURE) Act was enacted in 2019. It offers employers a chance to join multiple-employer plans and presents retirement options to employees. This can be a way to tie expenses to a rewarding option in the long run.

Before the SECURE Act, 401(k) or IRA account holders had to withdraw required minimum distributions (RMDs) in the year they turned over seventy and a half. The SECURE Act increased that age to seventy-two. It now begins at seventy-three if you were born between 1951 and 1959 and at seventy-five if you were born in 1960 or after.

Depending on the tax bracket, there may be taxes depending on your income in the year you withdraw. The SECURE Act has also eliminated the maximum age for traditional IRA contributions, which was previously capped at seventy and a half years old.

Max Out Retirement Accounts and Contributions

Similar to taxable income, contributions can also be maximized by $22,500 for a 401(K) or 403(b) plan for the year 2023. Those fifty and above can receive over $7,500 in tax breaks, whereas younger can do so for $6,500. Any income utilized well from tax is income protected and extended.

So, if you, your employees, or your family do not have a retirement plan, then you should contribute to an individual retirement account (IRA). Taxpayers who do have workplace retirement plans (or whose spouses do) may be able to deduct some or all of their traditional IRA contribution from taxable income, depending on their income.

Other Benefits

Employers can offer other plans to exclude contributions from tax income. Employee W-2 statements can appear under non-taxed amounts. Benefits can range from education assistance to expense reimbursements and life insurance.

A Health-Savings Account (HAS) can also be offered or availed by those who have a high-deductible health insurance plan. This can lead to reduced taxes and lead to reduced taxable income. An added benefit is that qualified medical expenses are withdrawn with no tax.

Over time, these contributions can continue to grow without having a requirement to pay tax on them. So, how else will you extend your income other than to maximize your tax-exempt contributions? The answer is by claiming tax credits such as those on earned income, COVID-19, and child benefits.

As per the tax year 2023, a low-income taxpayers can claim credits up to $7,430 if there are three or more children in the qualifying age and bracket. It reduces to under four thousand with one child. Even if there are no children, around six hundred can be claimed in tax credits. The Child and Dependent Care Credit can, depending on income, help offset qualified expenses for the care of children and disabled dependents.

The American Opportunity Tax Credit offers up to twenty-five per year for eligible students for the first four years of higher education. The Lifetime Learning Credit, on the other hand, has a maximum of twenty percent credit for up to $10,000 of qualified expenses or $2,000 per return.

There is also the Saver's Credit for moderate and lower-income individuals. This is for those aiming to save for retirement. Under the plan, individuals can receive a credit of up to half their contributions to a plan. So why would the IRS allow you to deduct and save on paying taxes?

Conclusion

The IRS allows you to deduct quite a few items, so you do not have to overburden yourself with taxes and end up losing revenue or harming your business. Similarly, for those employed, extra expenses can be covered, and childcare can be improved through the use of tax-exempt funds and deductions.

This is known as the lowering of a tax drag. You can maximize your after-tax wealth. The issue is that even smaller drags can continue to have a huge impact in the long run. Let's consider an example to understand the effect.

If there is a hundred-thousand in retirement investments over ten years, then a final amount of double the amount will not be achieved with the promised 7.5% return per annum. This would be due to a two-percent tax drag. While tax rates vary over time, it is important to understand that investments not handled smartly can be harmful for the financial health of a company.

While it is important to pay taxes owed, it should be done smartly, and no one should have to pay more if they can save their money legally. If you spend a few hours on the IRS website, IRS.gov, and rely on verified financial information, then you save yourself and your business hundreds of thousands of dollars in tax savings.

This is why, whenever possible, you should have a look at online and authentic information and consult qualified tax professionals to prepare and file your returns. At the very least, you can try to obtain free and basic consultation to gain tax assistance. Also, with tax software, consultation, and knowledge, you will be able to plan ahead and save in business deductions.

Chapter 21: Tax Planning Strategies

In a bid to minimize tax liabilities within a legal framework, individuals root for loopholes within the tax system where they could save on paying for additional taxes and realize additional income without paying any further amount. Tax planning involves analyzing financial circumstances, where individuals and organizations take advantage of available tax deductions, credits, exemptions, and incentives and make informed decisions to render tax savings. Effective tax planning can help save money and reduce the overall tax burden in several ways.

Tax planning allows individuals and businesses to take advantage of various tax deductions and credits. The process commences with carefully examining the tax code and understanding eligibility requirements. In this way, taxpayers can identify deductions and credits that apply to their specific situation. Common deductions include expenses related to education, healthcare, mortgage interest, and charitable contributions. Tax credits are useful tools for a reduction in tax liability and can be valuable for those planning to save on taxes. By maximizing deductions and credits, taxpayers can significantly lower their taxable income, resulting in lower tax bills.

The whole process is based on the strategic timing of income and expenses. By deferring income to a later year or scaling deductions of the current year, individuals and businesses can modify their taxable income levels. For example, deferring the receipt of a year-end bonus means that the associated tax liability for the particular bonus would be due for the next year. Similarly, making business purchases before year-end can allow for immediate deductions. By carefully planning the timing of income and expenses, taxpayers can effectively manage their tax liabilities and potentially save money.

Individuals and businesses also align investment strategies with tax planning to yield tax advantages. There are many platforms where individuals and businesses can source tax advantages, such as Individual Retirement Accounts (IRAs) or 401(k) plans. They allow individuals to defer taxes on investment earnings until they withdraw the amount during retirement. Contributions to these accounts may also be tax-deductible, further reducing current tax liabilities. Also, tax planning involves evaluating investment options for tax efficiency. For instance, investing in tax-free municipal bonds can provide income that is exempt from federal taxes. By choosing tax-efficient investments, taxpayers can optimize their returns after tax, potentially reducing their tax burden.

Tax planning involves taking advantage of available tax incentives and exemptions.

Governments often offer incentives to promote certain behaviors of industries. For example, tax credits may be available for adopting renewable energy systems or investing in research and development. Leveraging these incentives allows individuals and businesses to not only save money but also contribute to societal or environmental goals. Similarly, tax planning involves utilizing exemptions. Certain types of organizations are deemed to have tax-exempt status, or there are tax-free natures of certain types of income. By understanding and utilizing these exemptions, taxpayers can minimize their tax liabilities legally.

Changing your tax status can potentially help you save money and reduce your tax liability. Your filing status determines the tax rates and deductions available for you or your organization. For example, if you're currently single but get married, you may be eligible to file jointly with your spouse. Filing jointly can often result in a lower tax liability compared to filing independently, especially if one spouse earns more than the other. In contrast, getting divorced or being legally separate allows you to file your tax return as head of household, usually provided with more favorable tax rates than filing as single. Changing your tax status may make you eligible for additional deductions and tax credits and can also impact your ability to contribute to retirement savings accounts. For example, if you switch jobs or become self-employed, you may gain access to different retirement plans, such as a 401(k) or a Simplified Employee Pension (SEP) IRA. There are certain tax statuses that come with additional exemptions and allowances. For example, if you're a senior citizen or have a disability, you may be eligible for additional tax exemptions or deductions. Changing your tax status to reflect your current circumstances can ensure that you take advantage of these benefits.

Pass-through entities, such as sole proprietorships, partnerships, Limited Liability Companies (LLCs), and S corporations, have the potential to save money and taxes in certain situations compared to profit-oriented corporations (C corporations). Pass-through businesses are not subjected to federal income tax; they report their income on individual tax returns of their owners, taxed at particular rates. They do not pay taxes at the entity level. Instead, the profits or losses are shifted to the owners' personal tax returns, and they are taxed at the individual tax rates. This avoids the issue of double taxation that occurs in C corporations, where profits are taxed at the corporate level and then again taxed when distributed to shareholders as dividends.

The QBI deduction introduced as part of the Tax Cuts and Jobs Act of 2017 allows pass-through business owners to deduct up to 20% of their qualified business income from their taxable income. The deduction is subjected to certain limitations but can result in substantial tax savings for eligible taxpayers. Pass-through entities often have more flexibility in deducting business losses than C corporations. Losses from a pass-through entity can offset the owner's other sources of income. Therefore, it reduces their overall tax liability. In contrast, C corporations cannot pass losses through to their shareholders. They are usually carried forward to offset future profits within the corporation. Not having to pay taxes at the entity level means that profits are only taxed once, at the individual level, and the owners can generally retain more after-tax income compared to a C corporation. Lastly, pass-through entities often have simpler administrative and reporting requirements required by law as compared to C corporations. This can result in lower compliance costs, reducing the administrative burden of managing the entity's tax affairs.

Conclusion

Tax planning strategies are widely recognized for helping people to save from stringent taxation systems. They enable financial experts to devise more comprehensive and legally compliant strategies to help people dodge the taxation system and get an enhanced return on their income. However, amidst their money-saving prospects, they still allow individuals and businesses to save on their money up to a limited extent. Tax loopholes provide temporary relief from a liability that has to be paid at any time in the future. Although COVID-19 offered a huge relief for organizations, these are exceptional circumstances and can't be relied upon as prolonged merits.

Step 6: Wealth Accumulation and Protection System

Chapter 22: Introduction

Many people stress themselves out their entire lives working on wages for average sustenance. There is no doubt that these people want to enjoy a better life but are uninformed about the roadmap that allows them to build their wealth. Similarly, most businesses seem to survive only on short-term funding, which is not enough to attain growth. It becomes evident that most of them don't have a full-fledged plan in place that enables them to build their wealth accordingly. Those who successfully manage to scale their wealth follow a well-defined wealth accumulation plan to comply with their growth objectives.

A wealth accumulation plan is a strategic approach to building and expanding one's wealth over time. It involves setting clear financial goals and implementing effective strategies for savings and investments to maximize the growth of their assets. A wealth accumulation plan is primarily aimed at generating wealth and increasing financial resources to pursue various long-term objectives. These long-term goals may involve retirement planning, purchasing a home, or starting a business. A wealth accumulation plan is typically defined as a blend of different strategies, such as saving money, investing in various types of assets, and managing risk.

To create a wealth accumulation plan, you initially need to define your financial goals and objectives. This could include determining the level of wealth you want to achieve, the desired income levels, or specific milestones you wish to reach. Then, you proceed to establish a budget that tracks your income, expenses, and savings. By allocating a portion of your income toward savings, you can build a strong foundation for allocating funds for investment opportunities.

Managing your debt is also a crucial aspect of a wealth accumulation plan. You can assess and effectively manage your business's existing debts, such as loans, payables, mortgages, debentures, etc. In addition, you can also reduce your financial burden by freeing up funds for investments and savings. Additionally, it is fundamental to determine an appropriate asset allocation strategy. This involves deciding how to distribute your investments across different classes of assets, such as stocks, bonds, real estate, or alternative investments. Asset allocation should be based on your risk management and financial goals.

Developing an investment strategy that aligns with your risk profile and long-term objectives is crucial. This may involve diversifying your investments across various platforms. You may invest in different industries, geographical regions, or financial assets or securities, such as stocks, mutual funds, or real estate. It is important for your business to consistently contribute funds to your investment portfolio or other wealth-building platforms. Regular contributions, combined with the power of compound interest, can significantly accelerate wealth accumulation over time.

Risk management is another crucial aspect of a wealth accumulation plan. It is a part of protecting your wealth, involving the purchase of insurance policies, such as life insurance, health insurance, or disability insurance, to protect your wealth and mitigate financial risks. Therefore, it is important to regularly review and adjust your wealth accumulation plan to ensure that you don't deviate from your track. So, monitor your business's progress toward its goals, evaluate investment performance, and make necessary adjustments as circumstances change.

How a Wealth Accumulation Plan Works

A wealth accumulation plan can involve a formal arrangement with an investor who periodically contributes a significant amount of money to fund a business. This type of arrangement is commonly seen in investment partnerships, joint ventures, or private equity businesses. It allows individuals or businesses to systematically invest their capital into a business over time, with the prime aim of accumulating wealth and generating returns on their investment.

In such a plan, the investor commits to contributing funds at regular intervals. The arrangement is predetermined and agreed upon in a formal contract or partnership agreement. The contributions can take various forms, such as equity investments, loans, or convertible debt. The periodic nature of this funding ensures there's a consistent capital injection into the business that later supports its growth and expansion objectives. By following a wealth accumulation plan, the investor takes advantage of the potential upside of the business's success. As the business progresses, it will continue to generate profits, increase its valuation, or provide dividends or distributions to investors. This allows the investor's wealth to grow over time as they accumulate returns on their initial investments.

The periodic injections of capital provide a stable and predictable source of funding, reducing reliance on external funding or the need for attaining frequent fundraising activities. This can enhance the business's financial stability, enable strategic initiatives, and fuel its growth.

Furthermore, the formal arrangement provides clarity and structure to the investor-business relationship. It outlines the rights, responsibilities, and obligations of both parties, establishing a framework for decision-making, profit-sharing, and potential exit strategies. In this way, the interests of the investor and the business are aligned, promoting a collaborative and mutually beneficial partnership.

However, it's important to note that implementing a wealth accumulation plan requires careful consideration and due diligence. Investors should thoroughly evaluate the business's current situation, identified through the assessment of various factors, such as the business's management team, market conditions, and associated risks, before committing their capital. They should also consult legal and financial professionals to ensure the arrangement is properly structured, compliant with regulations, and aligned with their investment objectives.

The process of wealth accumulation usually involves setting specific goals, developing a comprehensive savings and investment strategy, and regularly monitoring and adjusting the plan as needed. For a business, the main objective of a wealth accumulation plan is to increase the entity's resources and achieve long-term financial security.

The first step in forming a wealth accumulation plan is to set specific financial goals. These goals may include increasing revenue and profitability, expanding market share, funding research and development activities, acquiring new assets or technologies, or diversifying the company's product or service portfolio. By identifying these goals, the business can determine the amount of wealth it needs to accumulate to create a roadmap to achieve those objectives.

Once these goals are established, the business can formulate a savings and investment strategy. This strategy may involve allocating a portion of the company's profits toward retained earnings that can be reinvested back into the business to take advantage of future growth opportunities. It also encompasses identifying appropriate investment platforms, such as stocks, bonds, or other financial instruments, to generate additional returns on excess cash reserves.

Businesses need to regularly monitor and adjust their wealth accumulation plan. This includes reviewing their final accounts, assessing key performance indicators (KPIs), and analyzing the company's overall financial health. By tracking progress and identifying areas for improvement, businesses can make informed decisions to enhance their wealth portfolio. The business may later readjust its strategies by reallocating resources, diversifying investment portfolios, or exploring new growth opportunities.

Alongside the wealth accumulation plan, a robust protection system is essential to safeguard a business's accumulated wealth. A wealth protection system for a business usually includes comprehensive strategies such as risk management, insurance coverage, and contingency planning. A business practicing risk management identifies and assesses potential risks that could impact the company's financial stability and implements strategies to mitigate those risks.

This may entail performing risk assessments, creating business continuity plans, enforcing internal controls and compliance protocols, and staying abreast of industry trends to mitigate emerging risks.

Insurance can significantly help in protecting a business's wealth, depending on the nature of the business. The insurance coverage may include property and casualty insurance to protect physical assets, liability insurance to cover potential legal claims, and key person insurance to mitigate the financial impact of losing key individuals within the organization.

Lastly, a business establishes a contingency plan to handle unforeseen events or crises that could disrupt operations and impact its financial stability. This may include creating recovery plans for disastrous events, setting up emergency funds or lines of credit, and implementing succession plans to ensure continuity in case of leadership changes or unexpected departures.

Key Aspects of Wealth Accumulation

- **Capital Accumulation Plan (CAP)** : While a wealth accumulation plan for a business has a broader focus and involves strategies to increase the overall wealth or value of the business, a capital accumulation plan typically refers to the process of accumulating funds or capital within the business for specific purposes. This can involve setting aside funds for business expansion, investment in new equipment or technology, research and development activities, or other ventures requiring significant injections of capital. The emphasis is on accumulating capital within the business to support its growth, operations, and strategic objectives. It often involves generating profits, retaining earnings, and reinvesting them into the business. In essence, a capital accumulation plan is more specific and focuses on accumulating capital within the business for particular purposes. In comparison, a wealth accumulation plan takes a more comprehensive approach to increasing the overall value and wealth of the business by considering various factors that contribute to the business's financial well-being.

- **Voluntary Accumulation Plan:** A voluntary accumulation plan typically refers to a savings or investment program that allows employees or stakeholders of the business to voluntarily contribute their own funds toward building wealth or accumulating assets. It is an optional plan in which individuals can participate in addition to any mandatory retirement or savings programs provided by the business. A voluntary accumulation plan allows individuals to save and invest their own money according to their financial goals and preferences. It gives them greater control and flexibility over their wealth accumulation strategies, allowing them to optimize their contributions and investment choices to cater to their individual needs.

- **Dollar-cost Averaging:** Dollar-cost averaging is an investment strategy used in wealth accumulation for businesses. It involves the business consistently investing a fixed amount of money at regular intervals, regardless of the price or value of the investment. A fixed dollar amount is invested on a predetermined schedule, such as monthly or quarterly. This approach helps to mitigate the impact of market volatility and alternates the need to time the market or make investment decisions based on short-term fluctuations. With businesses investing a fixed amount regularly, they end up purchasing more shares or units of an investment when prices are lower and fewer shares or units when prices are higher. Over time, this strategy can result in a lower average cost per share or unit.

Benefits of a Wealth Accumulation Plan

A wealth accumulation plan can offer several benefits for a business:

- **Financial Security:** It helps businesses build a strong foundation and long-term security. By consistently saving and investing, the business can accumulate assets and resources that can be used to reduce economic downturns, fund expansion initiatives, or invest in new opportunities. It acts as a barrier against unexpected financial challenges and helps the business maintain stability.

- **Growth and Expansion:** A wealth accumulation plan, later on, generates capital for growth and expansion. By setting aside funds or investing in growth-oriented assets, a business can accumulate wealth that can be utilized for other profitable ventures, such as acquiring new assets, expanding operations, entering new markets, developing new products or services, or investing in research and development.

- **Capital for Investments :** It makes room for funds used for strategic investments. This could include investing in new equipment, technology upgrades, infrastructure development, or acquiring other businesses. Having a dedicated pool of accumulated wealth provides the business with the financial flexibility to seize opportunities that arise and make investments that can enhance future profitability and competitiveness.

Conclusion

It's important to note that a wealth accumulation plan should be tailored to your unique circumstances, goals, and risk tolerance. Seeking guidance from financial professionals, such as financial advisors or wealth managers, can provide valuable expertise in designing and implementing an effective wealth accumulation plan that suits your needs.

In conclusion, a wealth accumulation plan can involve a formal arrangement where an investor periodically contributes a significant amount of money to fund a business. This arrangement, often seen in investment partnerships or private equity structures, facilitates consistent capital injections and aims to generate wealth and returns on the investor's investment. It benefits both the investor and the business by supporting growth, enhancing financial stability, and establishing a clear framework for the partnership. Nonetheless, careful evaluation and professional guidance are essential to ensure the success and effectiveness of such a plan.

In summary, a wealth accumulation plan and protection system for a business work together to achieve financial growth and stability. The wealth accumulation plan focuses on increasing the company's net worth and achieving specific financial goals through savings, investments, and strategic decision-making. The protection system aims to mitigate risks and safeguard the accumulated wealth through risk management, insurance coverage, and contingency planning. Regular monitoring, adjustment, and adaptation are essential for both the wealth accumulation plan and the protection system to ensure the long-term financial well-being of the business.

Chapter 23: Rising Economic Inequity for Small Business

With the current income disparity in the United States, most small and medium enterprises are exposed to a multitude of challenges. Consumer expenditure has rapidly decreased with limited access to funding. There is a massive shortage of skilled labor in the market, particularly for the latter reason. Entrepreneurship is not the same anymore, with the government overregulating the business industry, coupled with heightening political pressures. The situation has become dire to such an extent that there is a grave need to support small businesses in order to cater to a more inclusive and resilient economy. As wealth becomes increasingly concentrated in the hands of a few, small businesses often face several challenges that can hinder their growth and sustainability.

A large portion of the population struggles with low wages and stagnant income growth, with their purchasing power gradually diminishing. As a result, small businesses, which heavily rely on local customers, are experiencing a decline in sales revenue. That could have adverse after-effects, as reduced consumer spending can further enhance economic inequality, creating even more financial strain for small businesses.

Small businesses also need access to funding and credit to fuel their running expenses. Large corporations and wealthy individuals already seem to have easier access to capital. Still, small businesses that are owned by small-time entrepreneurs whose business is located in low-income areas may face difficulties in securing loans or investments. Therefore, innovation and expansion could be off the table. They would struggle to compete with larger, more established companies.

They also struggle to maintain a desirable workforce resulting from widening income disparity. The majority of qualified and skilled workers seek higher-paying opportunities, largely offered by huge corporations. This can lead to talent shortages for small businesses. It makes it difficult for them to attract and retain skilled employees, further reducing their ability to grow and stay competitive.

The United States government has also recently increased regulation and taxation on businesses. As the wealth gap widens, there may be growing public pressure and demand for policies addressing income inequality. Small businesses could become targets for policymakers who seek to redistribute wealth or raise revenue through increased taxes and regulations. These additional burdens may excessively exploit the resources of small businesses, making it harder for them to expand and create jobs.

Overall, the competitive landscape is drastically threatened. When larger corporations gather significant wealth, they may use their financial advantage to engage in unethical pricing strategies. It would directly threaten the survival of small businesses. Market monopolization and reduced choices in goods and services shall be the most obvious consequences, ultimately limiting consumer choices and negatively affecting the economy's overall health.

The Pandemic Effect

The COVID-19 pandemic exposed the fragility of small businesses. Everyone knows that it has had a profound and lasting impact on small businesses worldwide. While some businesses managed to adapt and endure in this challenging time, many others faced unprecedented challenges that left them more fragile than ever before.

The pandemic instigated widespread lockdowns, with governments complying with social distancing measures. This resulted in a significant drop in the number of global customers. Many small businesses heavily rely on in-person interactions and local customers. With restrictions in place, physical traffic declined sharply, leading to a sharp decline in revenue and financial strain. Some businesses, particularly those in the hospitality and retail industry, struggled to keep their doors open, eventually leading to closures and job losses.

Supply chains were affected on a global scale. Unlike large corporations, small businesses often lack the resources and bargaining power, making them more vulnerable to supply chain disruptions. Many small businesses depend on goods and materials from other countries, but travel restrictions and factory closures in response to the pandemic disrupted the flow of products, resulting in inventory shortages and delays. This affected their ability to meet customer demands and increased their operational costs.

The lockdown prompted businesses to shift to remote work, which presented unique challenges for small businesses. Unlike larger corporations with established infrastructure, small businesses often lack the resources and expertise to transition smoothly to transition to remote work transition to remote work. This sudden shift caused communication gaps and increased cybersecurity risks. It made them more susceptible to operational inefficiencies and potential data breaches.

Access to an adequate amount of capital became a major issue for small businesses during the pandemic. Many of them struggled to secure loans or financial support from the government, as they rendered complicated application processes to discourage lending. Consequently, these businesses found it challenging to maintain their operations, pay employees, and cover fixed expenses, further contributing to their fragility.

Businesses also witnessed a significant shift in consumer behavior as people started embracing online shopping and digital services at an unprecedented rate. The behavior favored larger e-commerce platforms and established brands over smaller, local businesses. As a result, many small businesses experienced reduced demand and lost market share to larger competitors, further weakening their financial position.

The pandemic highlighted the importance of adapting to technology. Small businesses that were slow to adapt to the digital landscape found themselves at the back of the queue. Those without a strong online presence struggled to reach customers effectively, which reduced sales and brand visibility.

Small businesses also had to comply with evolving health and safety regulations. It meant that they had to invest in safety equipment, implement social distancing measures, and adhere to strict guidelines, involving further exhaustion of their financial resources.

The pandemic also impacted small business owners' and employees' mental health and well-being. The stress and uncertainty surrounding the crisis affected their ability to make critical decisions. Hence, they had difficulty maintaining motivation, potentially leading to burnout and reduced productivity.

The Dominance of Big Players

The key players in various industries have a significant impact on both consumers and workers of small businesses. This phenomenon refers to the increasing dominance of a few large companies in a particular market. As a consequence of reduced competition, consumers are left with limited choices, as society in general also has to pay for deteriorating pricing, quality, and employment opportunities.

For consumers, the dominance of big firms can lead to reduced options and less competitive pricing. As larger corporations acquire smaller businesses or gain significant market power, they can influence prices and dictate terms more effectively, hence leaving consumers with fewer choices. With fewer competitors in the market, there is no rationale for big firms to offer lower prices, high-quality products, or innovative services. This lack of competition can lead to higher prices and reduced product diversity. It limits consumer access to affordable and varied goods and services.

Innovation becomes one of the main victims in these circumstances. Smaller businesses often drive creativity and competition by introducing new products or services that cater to specific needs. However, when large firms dominate the market, they are less motivated to invest in research and development or take risks with new ideas. Then, consumers experience slower technological advancements and a lack of innovation compared to a more competitive marketplace with diverse players.

As larger corporations expand and dominate the market, they may engage in cost-cutting measures. This move implicates potential job losses and reduced job security for workers of small businesses. With fewer small businesses to provide employment opportunities, workers find it increasingly challenging to find jobs that align with their skills and interests.

This gives us an outlook on the bargaining power they have over their employees. When a few dominant companies control a significant portion of the job market, workers may have limited alternatives and may be forced to accept unfavorable working conditions or lower salaries. The imbalance in bargaining power reduces a worker's ability to negotiate fair wages, benefits, and job security.

The concentration of big firms can also have a broader impact on the economy and local communities. Small businesses often contribute to the diversity and vibrancy of local economies. They provide unique goods and services and promote a sense of community. However, when big firms consolidate their power, they may prioritize their bottom line over community interests, leading to potential disinvestment in local areas and reduced support for community initiatives.

With dominant players controlling key markets, newcomers also find it challenging to enter the industry and compete effectively. This lack of competition stifles entrepreneurship and reduces economic dynamism, potentially hindering long-term economic growth and job creation.

Small Businesses and Diversity

Race, gender, and ethnicity have emerged as significant determinants of success in small businesses. Despite progress in promoting diversity and inclusion, disparities continue to exist. This has affected small businesses' access to resources, funding, market opportunities, and networking, whereas these factors have a profound impact on the success and growth of small businesses, making it essential for them to address these inequalities for a more equitable entrepreneurial landscape.

Studies have shown that entrepreneurs from certain racial and ethnic backgrounds, such as Black, Hispanic, or Indigenous, face various challenges in accessing capital and resources compared to their white counterparts. Discrimination and biases within the financial sector can result in limited access to loans, credit, and venture capital. It reduces their chances of expansion and development. As a result, minority-owned businesses may struggle to scale up and compete on an equal footing.

Particularly when it comes to female entrepreneurs, racial disparities exist in the business landscape. Women often encounter obstacles in accessing funding and support networks, facing stereotypes and unconscious biases that limit their opportunities. This can lead to the underrepresentation of women in certain industries and leadership roles, which affects their ability to succeed and grow their small businesses. Encouraging gender diversity and implementing policies promoting equal opportunities for women entrepreneurs is crucial to establishing a thriving entrepreneurial ecosystem.

In this case, immigrant entrepreneurs may also face unique challenges, including language barriers, cultural differences, and navigating complex legal processes. They generally contribute significantly to small business formation and innovation. Their success highlights the importance of supporting and empowering this diverse segment of entrepreneurs. Creating inclusive programs and initiatives that cater to the needs of immigrant entrepreneurs can enhance their chances of succeeding in their business ventures.

The impact of race, gender, and ethnicity on networking and market opportunities cannot be underestimated. In many industries, well-established networks and connections are crucial for business growth and access to new customers. However, these networks can be exclusive, making it challenging for individuals from underrepresented backgrounds to penetrate these circles. Lack of access to key networks can limit market reach and visibility, affecting the ability of small businesses owned by marginalized groups to thrive and expand.

Addressing these disparities requires a multi-faceted approach in which policymakers must implement measures that promote equitable access to capital, resources, and business support services. This may involve creating targeted funding programs, providing mentorship opportunities, and promoting financial literacy in marginalized communities.

Furthermore, diversity and inclusion should be prioritized in all aspects of the entrepreneurial ecosystem, from startup accelerators and incubators to industry conferences and networking events. Encouraging collaboration and partnerships between businesses owned by underrepresented groups and established players can also create more opportunities for growth and market access.

Diversity and inclusivity have become important elements of success in small businesses. The disparities entrepreneurs face from marginalized backgrounds in accessing funding, networks, and market opportunities hampers their ability to thrive and grow their ventures. To foster a more inclusive and equitable entrepreneurial landscape, addressing these challenges through targeted policies is essential. Entities should opt for increased diversity and a concerted effort to break down barriers that limit access to resources and opportunities. By creating a more level playing field, society can unlock the full potential of diverse entrepreneurs and promote sustainable economic growth.

Conclusion

The competitive landscape has drastically changed for small businesses. The post-pandemic situation has exposed these entities to several challenges that they could not begin to navigate through. With global supply chain problems followed by increased adaptivity to technology, small and medium enterprises are facing stringent difficulties in keeping up with the recent trends. Above that, the key players in the market, which are comparatively well off in adapting themselves to these situations, continue to adapt more to these challenges. Making small businesses compete with them barely. Even though they have followed certain contemporary practices, such as promoting diversity in workplaces, they face difficulty keeping themselves aligned with the objectives when their survival is threatened.

Chapter 24: CARES Act

Small businesses hold tremendous significance in balancing the prevailing inequalities within societies. Where a society is characterized by an unfair wealth distribution and limited access to opportunities, small businesses seem to cure that imbalance with their entrepreneurial ethic. Evidently, they are very useful in tackling various social and economic challenges.

Small businesses are significant engines of job creation, particularly at the local level. They are usually labor-intensive enterprises that often hire from the communities they operate in. They provide employment opportunities to a diverse workforce sourced from different backgrounds. Hence contributing toward reduced income disparity and lifting people out of poverty.

You may see them more inclined toward inclusive hiring practices. They can be more open to hiring individuals from disadvantaged backgrounds, such as those with limited formal education or work experience. Embracing diversity in their workforce enables these businesses to bridge the opportunity gap, offering a way for people to improve their economic circumstances.

They provide opportunities for aspiring entrepreneurs to establish their ventures, allowing them to move from lower-income positions to higher-income ones. This mobility can break the cycle of poverty. It gives the grounds to promote innovation in line with generating more equitable economic outcomes.

Local wealth generation is at play when left to these small businesses. When people support small, local businesses, a greater portion of the revenue remains within the community. This circulation stimulates economic growth and creates a multiplier effect. Hence, it minimizes the wealth disparities within the region.

Small businesses also actively participate in community development. They often have a vested interest in the welfare of their communities. They engage in initiatives like sponsoring local events and supporting social causes. It helps them to build stronger, more resilient communities and reduces social inequalities.

By offering goods and services tailored to the needs of the local population, small businesses address the shortage of essential products in the market. Their presence can increase accessibility and affordability, especially in underserved areas. Other than just the provision of necessary products, they are also found to promote economic diversification by offering a wide range of products and services. This diversification can help reduce reliance on a few dominant industries or corporations. Additionally, it creates more opportunities for individuals to participate in various economic activities. They also boost innovation and competition in their local region, leading to more affordable and higher-quality products and services. This is particularly beneficial for lower-income consumers, as it provides them with better choices at competitive prices.

Small businesses also have the potential to promote financial inclusion by providing opportunities for individuals with limited access to traditional banking services to participate in the economy. They may accept cash payments or offer informal credit options. This renders multiple economic opportunities for underserved populations.

Equality Across Ethnicity and Gender

Rather than just catering to economically sidelined groups, small businesses act as support groups for various ethnicities and gender inequalities within societies. They adopt inclusive practices in which they maintain a diverse and equitable work environment where they can contribute to breaking down barriers and creating a more equal society.

Firstly, they emphasize fair and unbiased hiring practices. They often adopt blind recruitment processes that focus on skills, qualifications, and experience rather than names or ethnic backgrounds.

This practice helps to ensure that individuals from different ethnicities have equal opportunities to secure employment and advance their careers.

Small businesses have the potential to create a welcoming and inclusive workplace culture that celebrates diversity. By valuing the unique perspectives and experiences of employees from various ethnic backgrounds, they give their members a sense of belonging and appreciation. This, in turn, enhances creativity, innovation, and overall employee satisfaction, which can benefit the company's performance.

Across their organization, they also support and collaborate with suppliers and partners from diverse backgrounds. Some of them are found to actively work with minority-owned businesses, where they contribute to the economic empowerment of underrepresented communities. This approach assists in building more inclusive supply chains and business networks.

In addition to promoting ethnic equality, small businesses can also play a significant role in advancing gender equality. They initiate by addressing gender biases in their hiring practices and promotion processes. They ensure that candidates are evaluated solely on their merits, regardless of their gender. They can offer flexible work arrangements, such as remote work options or flexible hours, to support work-life balance for all employees. This can be particularly beneficial for women who often face additional responsibilities related to caregiving and household tasks.

Another essential aspect is promoting women to leadership positions within the organization. Small businesses help break through the glass ceiling and achieve gender equality in leadership roles. In fact, they set an example for the industry and challenge the notion that certain positions are reserved for one gender.

They also conduct regular pay equity reviews to ensure that men and women are compensated fairly for the same work or work of equal value, thereby dissolving pay gap issues.

What is more, it is possible that they can implement policies against discrimination, harassment, and bias. They can prioritize creating a safe and respectful work environment for all employees, where they can help combat harmful stereotypes and promote gender equality.

Paycheck Protection Program

The Paycheck Protection Program (PPP) was a central component of the CARES Act. The PPP was designed to provide financial relief to small businesses across the United States that were severely impacted by the pandemic. This program was targeted at preventing mass layoffs, supporting payroll expenses, and incentivizing businesses to retain their workforce during a time of unprecedented uncertainty and financial strain. The COVID-19 pandemic brought about significant challenges for businesses of all sizes, but small businesses were particularly vulnerable to this economic downturn. Many were forced to close their doors temporarily as they faced reduced consumer demand or confronted major disruptions in their supply chains. Consequently, millions of jobs were at risk, and the livelihoods of countless Americans were in jeopardy.

When the need was recognized to support these businesses and their employees, the American Congress swiftly devised the PPP as part of the broader CARES Act. The program sought to provide short-term financial assistance to eligible small businesses through forgivable loans. The loans were designed to cover specific operating expenses. They compensated for payroll costs for an 8-week period following the deposit. This enabled these businesses to continue paying their employees during the economic downturn.

The PPP was administered by the U.S. Small Business Administration (SBA) in collaboration with participating lenders. This included banks, credit unions, and other financial institutions. Other than small businesses, some self-employed individuals and independent contractors were also eligible to apply for PPP loans.

To qualify for a PPP loan, businesses needed to demonstrate that they had been operational before February 15, 2020, and had experienced economic hardship due to the COVID-19 pandemic. The loan amounts were calculated based on a formula that considered the business's average monthly payroll costs, including salaries, wages, tips, employee benefits, and certain taxes.

The PPP had a significant impact on small businesses across the country. Many businesses that received PPP loans managed to maintain their workforce and continue operations.

It provided much-needed stability during a time of absolute uncertainty. Businesses were able to keep their employees on the payroll and prevented mass layoffs, reducing the burden on state unemployment systems.

However, the implementation of the PPP also came with its fair share of challenges. As the demand for loans surged, there were reports of overwhelmed lenders, delays in loan processing, and confusion over eligibility and documentation requirements. Some larger businesses with access to other sources of funding initially received PPP loans. The government had to move toward policy changes to prioritize smaller businesses. The program underwent several rounds of funding, with additional legislation passed to replenish and refine the program.

Overall, the Paycheck Protection Program played an important role in providing critical financial support to small businesses during an extraordinary and challenging time. It served as a lifeline for many enterprises, enabling them to retain their workforce, cover essential expenses, and continue operations despite economic uncertainty. The program's impact extended beyond businesses to the broader economy. It helped stabilize communities, support consumer spending, and contribute to economic recovery.

The PPP also opened up important conversations about the role of government in supporting businesses during emergencies. It also highlighted the vital contributions of small businesses to the economy. It alternated the need for effective and efficient disaster relief programs that can respond swiftly to crises while ensuring that assistance reaches those most in need.

The Challenges

The Small Business Administration (SBA) faced numerous administrative challenges while implementing the PPP. The urgency of the economic relief required during the COVID-19 pandemic presented several obstacles for the agency.

- **Overwhelming Demand:** The SBA received an unprecedented volume of loan applications for the PPP and other programs. The massive influx of requests burdened the agency's existing infrastructure and systems. It led to delays in processing applications and difficulties in handling the high volume of inquiries from small business owners.

- **Rapid Policy Changes:** The evolving nature of the pandemic and the need for immediate responses required instant policy adjustments. As the circumstances changed, the SBA had to revise its guidelines and requirements, resulting in confusion among both lenders and borrowers.

- **Limited Staff and Resources:** The SBA faced staffing and resource limitations that impeded its ability to handle a huge volume of applications. The agency had to scale up its operations quickly to meet the needs of small businesses across the country. But this expansion also came with logistical challenges and time constraints.

- **Technology and Infrastructure Issues:** The SBA's existing technology infrastructure was not fully equipped to handle the massive number of loan applications and information processing required for the PPP. As a result, there were reported issues with application portals crashing, creating delays that caused frustration for applicants.

- **Eligibility and Documentation Challenges**: Determining eligibility and verifying documentation for loan applicants involved complex processes. The SBA had to ensure that funds reached those in genuine need while also preventing misuse or fraudulent claims, which required rigorous verification procedures.

Conclusion

Small businesses play a vital role in addressing various economic challenges. They promote equality by creating jobs, encouraging social mobility, supporting community development, and nurturing financial inclusion.

They also have the potential to be powerful advocates for ethnic and gender equality. Their actions can set positive examples for larger corporations and contribute to a meaningful change in society.

Evidently, the United States government made an admirable effort to address the challenges for small businesses through the CARES Act. While the PPP has come to an end, with new programs and policies taking its place, its legacy will persist in shaping future discussions about economic relief and recovery efforts in times of crisis. The experience gained from its implementation will be valuable in preparing for and responding to future emergencies. It ensured that businesses and workers had the support they needed during challenging times.

WINSTON THOMPSON, MBA, CPA

Step 7: A Health and Wellness System

Chapter 25: Introduction

In today's dynamic business environment, workplace health and wellness have become increasingly important. It is not just about profit margins and market share, but the happiness and well-being of your employees that companies aim to outrival in.

Since people concerned with creating a meaningful and sustainable society have grown increasingly dissatisfied with purely financial measures of progress, well-being has taken center stage.

This shift is reflected in the workplace, where business leaders are looking for a purpose for their organizations beyond maximizing return on capital and realizing that securing such a position in and of itself contributes to commercial success.

Many people today, including the investor community, view human capital management as a sign of a company's long-term prospects because an organization's and its employees' well-being are inextricably linked.

A growing body of research demonstrates which activities impact workplace wellbeing, both positively and negatively, but there are still many gaps. Employers will likely play an increasingly significant role in determining the state of the human condition as workplace well-being continues to rise on the business agenda in the 21st century.

Employee well-being refers to how a person's job affects their well-being and happiness. When a company prioritizes employee well-being, its employees tend to be happier and less stressed.

An employee's well-being is influenced by several factors, some of which are physical health, emotional health, financial health, psychological well-being, and social well-being. It is crucial to remember that employee well-being affects every aspect of working life, and as a result, it significantly affects employee retention, engagement, and business success.

This chapter introduces integrating an employee health and wellness system into your business strategy as a crucial part of your Roadmap For Success. Promoting employee well-being benefits not only the employees but also the organization. Stress can be reduced, and productive workplaces that benefit individuals and organizations can be created by promoting well-being.

A key enabler of employee engagement and organizational performance can be good health and well-being. We are here to help you along the way, understanding the importance of small businesses and the difficulties they face specifically.

The Importance of Employee Health and Wellness

The team is the foundation of success in small start-ups and expanding businesses, which is why the well-being of employees is crucial, and every company should make it a key component of their HR strategy. A productive, engaged, and loyal workforce is motivated and healthy. Such a team also has a favorable effect on your bottom line by lowering absenteeism and healthcare expenses.

Employees who are content and in good health at work are more productive and use sick days less frequently. Furthermore, putting your team's health and happiness first is more important than ever because an increasing number of people are taking time off to recover from stress, anxiety, and depression. Your company's culture will be strengthened by creating a work environment that your employees enjoy. This will also protect their wellbeing. When employees are happy at their jobs, it shows in their interactions with others, which, in turn, helps businesses succeed. The wellbeing of every employee should be a top priority, primarily if they're known for optimal performance and are taking the time off for a bereavement or sickness. It is essential to take care of your employees at their worst to make sure they are there for you, too, when you need them most.

A healthy workforce is less likely to get sick, which results in lower medical expenses and less absenteeism. Additionally, employees who feel appreciated and supported are more likely to remain loyal to their employers, which results in cost savings from training and recruitment.

The Benefits of Workplace Well-being Initiatives

Implementing or enhancing an employee wellness program can impact small business owners in ways they may not initially anticipate. Large, incentive-based wellness programs do not necessarily require substantial financial outlays. Implementing free or inexpensive wellness benefits will have benefits far beyond a simple financial payback.

You can develop and implement various remote and office well-being programs in your company that will significantly impact the lives of your employees with some brainstorming, creativity, and an employee experience solution. The most significant benefit of well-being initiatives is a productive and content workforce. Additionally, they produce fascinating outcomes like:

- **Enhances Employee Health:** By encouraging your staff to adopt healthy behaviors, you help them avoid health issues that could result in chronic disease. Healthy eating and exercise are encouraged through wellness programs, which lower the risk of long-term health issues and make employees feel more energized and content throughout the course of their workdays.

Your team's mental health can also benefit from a wellness program. Many businesses encourage staff to develop healthy eating habits and offer wholesome food on-site to promote this behavior. According to research, eating a balanced diet keeps you feeling energetic for longer and can also help you feel less anxious and depressed.

- **Increases Productivity:** According to research, healthier workers are more likely to be productive at work because they are better rested, more energized, and more driven to finish their tasks on time and to their fullest potential. Employees focus on maintaining healthy behaviors like exercise, which has been shown to improve sleep and boost productivity at work when they participate in wellness programs.

- **Enhances Employee Engagement:** Organizations that cultivate an environment prioritizing employee wellness typically have a more engaged workforce. Employees who participate in walking clubs, weight loss challenges, and other wellness programs feel closer to their coworkers and the business they work for. The likelihood that an employee will stay with the company for a long time can be increased by participating in these activities, which help to strengthen the bonds that employees have with one another and their managers.

- **Enhances Morale:** Employees who participate in wellness programs report higher levels of job satisfaction, which can boost the morale of the entire team. Employees who participate in wellness programs feel more supported in achieving their health and wellness objectives, which makes them feel more appreciated by their employers.

The workday can be made more interesting by wellness programs. Employee learning is facilitated by educational initiatives and wellness activities that inject a sense of fun into the workplace to encourage engagement and raise morale.

- **Lower Stress Levels:** Although there is stress in the workplace, a wellness program can help to lessen or even eliminate it. By creating a wellness program that is focused on reducing workplace stress, you can improve the performance of your team and employee retention.

- **Attendance Is Increased:** Wellness initiatives help to enhance employee wellbeing. Making your team members feel more invested in their work, improving their health, and reducing stress to the absolute minimum can improve their overall job satisfaction. Employees are more motivated to come to work and give their best work when they feel well and have a positive work environment, which boosts attendance across the board.

- **Enhances Teamwork:** Employees who collaborate effectively are more productive and produce better work. Since teamwork typically fosters better collaboration and the development of more original ideas, they also tend to be more creative. Employees can improve their relationships with one another, support one another, and hold one another accountable for their goals by participating in wellness programs together, especially team-based activities. Participating in wellness activities outside the office can also aid in building team unity and camaraderie, enhancing workplace communication and collaboration.

- **Reduces Healthcare Costs:** By lowering healthcare expenses, wellness initiatives can save a business money. Employees of a company are less likely to become ill or suffer an injury at work if their health is improved. Employees receive medical attention less frequently as a result, saving the company money on healthcare costs.

- **Enhances Employee Health Behaviors:** The objective of any wellness program is to alter and improve employee behaviors. You can assist your team members in lowering their health risks and acquiring healthy habits that will improve all facets of their lives by enhancing workplace behaviors.

Research demonstrates that wellness initiatives can motivate staff to quit smoking, eat better, exercise more, and handle stress skillfully. Wellness initiatives have also been demonstrated to help workers lessen and better manage the symptoms of depression, thereby enhancing their general well-being.

- **Brings in Fresh Talent:** Prospective employees are curious about the additional benefits an employer provides in addition to salary. According to research, wellness programs are frequently listed among the benefits that job candidates say are very important to them. Wellness screenings, gym membership reimbursement, on-site clinics, initiatives to serve healthy options at an on-site canteen, and health and wellness competitions are some of the wellness benefits businesses provide.

You can entice more qualified candidates with a compensation package that includes wellness benefits. Businesses can use these wellness initiatives to foster strong loyalty among their staff members and boost long-term retention.

Steps to Incorporating Health and Wellness in the Workplace

By implementing wellness programs, small business owners can foster a caring and encouraging workplace environment. This improves productivity and overall success while also enhancing the health and happiness of their staff. Your team can achieve a healthy work-life balance, allowing them to succeed professionally and personally. Take into account these essential steps for a successful integration of a health and wellness system into your business plan:

1. Administering Health Risk Assessments

Health risk assessments are a great place to start on your path to a healthier workplace. These evaluations aid in locating any potential health problems that may exist among your staff. They reveal where your team stands in terms of their well-being. Recognize the health status of your staff before anything else. Health risk analyses can offer helpful insights into their requirements and potential improvement areas.

2. Paying People to Change Their Habits

Encourage positive behavior changes. If employees try to improve their well-being, think about rewarding or recognizing them. To encourage positive lifestyle changes, take into account implementing incentives. It is possible to increase employees' productivity and well-being over the long term by encouraging them to adopt healthier lifestyles. Gift cards or extra vacation time are examples of small incentives that can have a significant impact.

3. Sending People to Your Health Plan's Website

Utilize the tools provided by your health plan. Direct staff members to relevant online tools and resources so they can learn more about their health and wellness. Encourage your staff to browse the health plan website to learn more about the wealth of resources available. They can learn about wellness initiatives, preventive care, and other topics from this helpful resource.

4. Introducing Short-term Campaigns

Start short-term wellness challenges or campaigns to encourage good habits. These can be entertaining and stimulating, which will help your team bond. These campaigns may target health objectives like weight loss, physical fitness, or stress reduction. Ensure that they are enjoyable, engaging, and connected to practical goals.

5. Hiring a Vendor to "Fix" Unhealthy Employees

Think about collaborating with wellness companies that are experts at enhancing employee health. They can offer guidance and specially designed programs. Although promoting your employees' health is essential, remember that real change originates from within. Focus on empowering unhealthy employees rather than trying to "fix" them. Give them resources, advice, and tools that encourage them to take responsibility for their well-being.

6. Leadership Commitment and Support

A leader's commitment is essential as the leader sets the tone. Set an example for the entire organization by demonstrating your dedication to employee well-being. By setting an example, you can demonstrate your commitment to a healthier workplace. Encourage other leaders to follow suit to establish a wellness culture from the top down.

7. Building a Culture of Health

Establish a culture of wellness and health within the company. Promote open dialogue and activities that enhance both physical and mental health. Create an environment where everyone values happiness. Integrate wellness into the culture of your business. And eventually, it becomes a natural part of daily work life when compassion and understanding is incorporated into the mix of your company culture.

8. Asking for Help

Acknowledge that you do not have to handle everything alone. Consult with experts or individuals with knowledge of workplace wellness. Never be afraid to ask specialists or health care providers for help. They can offer advice, modify programs to meet your particular requirements, and guarantee the success of your wellness initiatives.

9. Spreading the Word

It is crucial to communicate. Inform your staff regularly about the available wellness initiatives, tools, and success stories. Share information on developments, achievements, and chances for workers to partake in wellness activities on a regular basis. Keep everyone informed by using a variety of channels, such as emails, bulletin boards, or team meetings.

10. Offering Smart Incentives

Create rewards for your team that they will appreciate. These might include discounts on wellness-related items, flexible work schedules, or gym memberships. Ensure rewards are in line with objectives and results related to health when giving them out. Consider offering bonuses if you want to encourage people to participate regularly in wellness activities, complete health challenges, or reach milestones.

11. Measuring the Right Things

Do more than just track participation; pay attention to the results. Examine how your wellness programs are affecting the productivity, satisfaction, and overall health of your employees. It is crucial to monitor development. Measure key health metrics, absenteeism rates, and productivity improvements. Utilize this information to modify your wellness initiatives and show employees and management how they have a positive financial impact.

Always remember that improving workplace health is a continuous journey, not a final destination. You can promote a well-being culture that is advantageous to everyone involved and the small business as a whole with your commitment and the involvement of your staff. You can all work together to make the days ahead healthier, happier, and more successful.

Creating a Holistic Roadmap for Success: Integrating Health and Wellness

It is more than just a trend to include a health and wellness section in your Roadmap for Success; doing so will help to ensure the success of your small business. Your workforce will be more resilient to challenges if they are healthy, rest assured.

Along with financial growth, your comprehensive roadmap should consider your employees' personal and professional development. It creates an atmosphere where everyone can thrive, from your leadership team to entry-level employees.

Success in small business is not solely based on revenue and expansion. It is about fostering a positive environment where the welfare of your team comes first. A comprehensive road map for success includes a section specifically for health and wellness and financial objectives. On this journey, we will examine the significance of this section, its effective integration, and the potential transformation of your small business.

Integrating Health and Wellness into Your Roadmap

We have established the significance of health and wellness, so let us look at how to successfully incorporate this element into your success plan.

1. Evaluate Your Current Situation

Begin by assessing your existing wellness initiatives, if any, as well as the overall health of your organization. Consider factors such as employee engagement, health benefits, and safety precautions. Understanding your starting point is crucial for setting meaningful goals.

2. Establish Specific Goals

What you hope to accomplish with your wellness and health initiatives should be made very clear. These goals could be anything from lowering absenteeism to enhancing mental health support.

Establish SMART objectives: specific, measurable, achievable, relevant, and time-bound.

3. Develop a Holistic Wellness Plan

Create a comprehensive wellness program that addresses physical, mental, and emotional health. Consider providing resources such as gym memberships, mental health counseling, and stress management workshops. Customize the program to meet the specific needs and preferences of your workforce.

4. Leadership Commitment

Gain the support of your leadership team. It sends a strong message to the entire organization when leaders support wellness initiatives. Encourage senior executives to take a proactive role in their wellness.

5. Employee Engagement

Make sure to involve your staff in the process. To learn about their preferences and needs in terms of wellness, conduct surveys or hold discussions. By including them early on, you can make sure your initiatives are worthwhile and well-received.

6. Allocation of Budgets

Give your wellness program a budget. Even though it is an investment, the benefits in terms of increased productivity and lower healthcare costs frequently outweigh the costs.

7. Education and communication

Effectively inform your staff of the advantages of your wellness program. Inform people about resources, stress management, and healthy living regularly. Think about holding workshops and challenges to promote wellness among your staff.

8. Track Progress and Modify

Create a system to monitor your progress toward your wellness objectives. Review statistics like employee satisfaction, healthcare use, and absenteeism rates regularly. Utilize this information to inform any program changes you make.

9. Acknowledge and Praise

Reward and recognize staff members who actively engage in wellness activities and meet wellness objectives. Recognition is a strong motivator and strengthens your dedication to good health.

10. Holistic Advantages

If possible, look into all-encompassing benefits like flexible scheduling, mental health days, and on-site wellness centers. These services can greatly enhance the well-being of employees.

11. Continuous Development

The pursuit of wellness is ongoing. Always look for ways to make your program better. Keep up with the newest developments and recommended procedures in workplace wellness.

Conclusion

It is not just a nice-to-have extra; incorporating health and wellness into your success plan is a strategic necessity. By emphasizing employee well-being, you build a business that is stronger and more resilient and succeeds not only financially but also in the health and happiness of its workforce.

Therefore, as you embark on this journey, remember that success is multifaceted. The success of your team, the expansion of your company, and the positive difference you make in the lives of your workers are all essential considerations. When you embrace wellness, your small business will grow in ways you never imagined.

In conclusion, incorporating a system for employee health and wellness is a potent tool for boosting the success of your small business. It is an investment in the future of your group that will boost output, employee happiness, and overall profitability. Small companies like yours have a special chance to set a positive example and demonstrate that success is about more than just the figures on a balance sheet; it is also about the happiness of your most important resource, your employees.

Chapter 26: Wellness Strategies

This book's final chapter will explore wellness strategies especially suited for small business owners. We recognize that not every business owner has an unlimited budget for wellness initiatives, but that does not mean you should not give your employees' well-being a higher priority.

In light of rising healthcare costs, employers and employees are looking for ways to make these costs manageable. Benefits for preventive health and wellness are intended to support employees in maintaining or changing their behavior to improve their health and lower their risk of illness. Organizations hope to reduce long-term health costs by preventing or reducing the prevalence of health issues among their workforce.

Employers encourage a healthier, more productive work environment by giving workers the means and the educational resources to take charge of their wellness. The relationship between one's health and job satisfaction is further supported by well-executed programs' ability to lower healthcare costs, boost productivity, and improve employee retention.

Corporate wellness programs have become popular as more employers understand the value of supporting their employees' health and well-being. With a well-designed corporate wellness program, employee morale and productivity can be raised, absenteeism and turnover can be decreased, and healthcare costs can also be reduced. Although it often requires careful planning, implementation, and evaluation, developing a successful corporate wellness program is not always that complex.

Implementing Cost-efficient Wellness Strategies

Maintaining a contented, healthy, and productive workforce requires small business owners to prioritize employee wellness. While providing wellness programs is essential, it is also critical to do so in an economical way. Here are some practical strategies to ensure your employees' well-being without straining your budget:

1. **Encourage a Healthy Workplace Culture:** Create a setting that supports healthy decisions. This includes setting up designated areas for physical activity or relaxation, offering standing desks, and providing wholesome snacks in the workplace.

2. **Flexible Work Arrangements:** Take into account remote work opportunities or flexible work hours can reduce stress, and general well-being can be enhanced by allowing employees to balance their personal and professional lives.

3. **Educational Workshops and Seminars:** Organize in-person or online workshops or seminars on wellness. These can cover topics such as stress

management, nutrition, fitness, and mental health. Look for regional authorities who might offer their services for free or charge less for these sessions.

4. **Use Technology:** Look into low-cost wellness-based platforms or apps that offer guided exercise programs, meditation sessions, and nutrition monitoring. Some of these tools are cost-effective or available for free.

5. **Employee-led Initiatives:** Encourage staff to take the initiative in planning wellness events. This might entail starting jogging or walking clubs, organizing healthy recipe swaps, or scheduling group exercise classes.

6. **Community Partnerships:** Work with nearby fitness centers or wellness facilities to offer group membership or discounts. Partnerships with the community frequently result in more affordable options for your employees.

7. **Health Challenges and Competitions:** Hold healthy competitions or challenges among your employees. These can motivate employees to stay active and make healthier choices. Offer participants small rewards or acknowledgments.

8. **Mindfulness and Stress Reduction:** Encourage stress-reduction practices like yoga or meditation. Either hire instructors for sporadic training sessions or direct staff members to online resources.

9. Peer Support Groups: Promote the formation of peer support groups for staff members who are dealing with comparable wellness issues. These groups can offer inspiration, responsibility, and emotional support without charging extra.

10. Frequently Scheduled Health Screenings: Make arrangements for affordable health examinations or screenings at the workplace. Early detection of health problems can avert more serious and expensive issues later on.

11. Effectively Utilize Current Benefits: Ensure your employees are fully aware of the benefits available to them through their health insurance plans. This could involve access to telehealth services, mental health care, or preventive care coverage.

12. Feedback and evaluation: Keep track of your staff's needs and preferences in terms of wellness. Utilize this feedback to improve and hone your wellness initiatives gradually.

You can promote your employees' well-being without breaking the bank by using these cost-effective wellness strategies. Keep in mind that even modest, incremental changes can greatly impact workers' well-being and job satisfaction, which will result in a more motivated and effective workforce for your small business.

Motivating and Incentivizing Employee Benefit Utilization

As a small business owner, you probably provide your staff with a package of benefits in an effort to support their well-being. However, it is common for employees to underuse these resources due to a variety of factors, such as ignorance, time restraints, or simply failing to appreciate what is offered fully. Motivating and rewarding your staff can be a smart move to make sure they take full advantage of these benefits.

1. **Raise Awareness:** To start, make sure that your staff is aware of the perks you offer. Regularly inform employees about these benefits through various means, including emails, workplace posters, and corporate meetings. Emphasize the importance and possible effects on their well-being.

2. **Establish a Culture of Wellness:** Encourage a work environment where the value of well-being is emphasized. Encourage team conversations about fitness, wellness, and stress reduction. Employees are more inclined to adopt wellness initiatives if they observe their coworkers engaging in them.

3. **Individualized Wellness Plans:** Be aware that every employee has different demands in terms of wellness. Consider providing individualized wellness programs or consultations where workers can discuss their objectives and difficulties with a healthcare

expert. Employees can better comprehend how particular perks can benefit them directly with the use of these customized techniques.

4. Rewards and Incentives: Rewards and incentives can be effective motivators. Consider implementing a reward system for staff members who utilize their benefits on a regular basis. This could entail publicly applauding their accomplishments, providing gift cards, or setting up wellness-related competitions with alluring cash awards.

Discount Programs for a Healthier Lifestyle

Many businesses collaborate with big-name retailers to provide employee discount programs that encourage a healthier way of life. Discount programs for wellness benefits can be as simple or complex as the employer chooses, and they can take many different shapes. These programs may offer substantial savings on a variety of wellness-related costs, such as gym memberships, access to sports clubs, fitness classes, and nutrition information.

Some wellness benefits aid workers in managing chronic and preventable illnesses like obesity, high blood sugar, and elevated cholesterol. Other wellness perks include incentive programs to encourage staff to complete particular health and wellness tasks, like yearly health risk assessments, smoking cessation programs, or weight loss plans. Employers frequently provide employees with preventive health and wellness information through different channels, such as wellness publications or health fairs, to help raise awareness of wellness issues and give employees the tools they need to lead healthy lives. Aside from these common types of wellness benefits, employers may provide programs and activities such as a 24-hour nurse line, CPR and first-aid training, massage therapy services, onsite nap rooms, sick rooms, or medical clinics.

An organization should carefully weigh the benefits, costs, levels of employee participation, and potential legal issues before implementing a wellness program or initiative. Some popular wellness activities include the following:

1. **Clinics For Vaccinations:** Hosting or participating in a vaccination clinic is a simple way to start a workplace wellness program. Many employees already make their own arrangements for annual vaccinations, but an employer's support for vaccinations can make it easier for employees to get them and increase the number of employees who do. Employees may also benefit from this support program as they adjust to the idea that their employer can play a positive role in maintaining their health.

2. **Dietary Education:** In nutrition-focused wellness initiatives, focus is placed on issues like obesity (which affects organ function and mobility), salt intake (which affects blood pressure), and carbohydrate intake (which affects diabetes).

Larger companies with cafeterias can promote healthy eating by creating a variety of healthy menu options. On the other hand, smaller businesses can provide nutritious refreshments instead of the usual junk ones at employee meetings.

3. **Physical Activities And Programs:** Regular physical activity is another important aspect of wellness. Before and after work, as well as during lunch breaks and specified exercise breaks, the workplace can host walking or other low-impact aerobic exercise activities. These are less expensive options than paying for gym memberships or having a health club on site.

4. **Admissions To Fitness Centers And Club Membership:** Employers should be aware of the potential costs and liability risks associated with on-site fitness centers, including the following:

- Significant overhead expenses are required for the building and the equipment.
- Employees may need to be instructed on suitable workout routines by trained personnel.

- Having a fitness center on-site might only draw in employees who are already physically fit; those who are out of shape or frightened by the atmosphere of a health club won't gain anything from it.
- Employees who suffer an injury while exercising on the job can be entitled to workers' compensation.

Therefore, paying for staff subscriptions at fitness clubs can be a wise alternative strategy. Employees would definitely benefit from the provision of child care, a wider selection of aerobics programs, and more flexible hours of operation. There would be no obligation on the part of the organization.

5. Health Checkups: Blood pressure, total cholesterol, triglycerides, glucose, waist and hip size, weight, height, body fat percentage, and body mass index (BMI) are frequently measured during health checks. A person's total fitness can also be determined through an assessment of their aerobic capacity. Employees can compare their health to demographic averages using their screening results.

Screenings are conducted during working hours and usually last 15 to 20 minutes. In larger firms, health screenings might be offered by the employer's medical department. Organizations without access to medical facilities can schedule screenings with their healthcare professionals or one of the many growing wellness companies.

The way that employees view health screening programs may differ. Some employees may consider them an invasion of their privacy, while others may see them as a free health benefit.

6. Health Risk Evaluations: Health risk assessments have developed into valuable tools for assisting staff in understanding and beginning to take control of their health. However, it can be difficult to persuade staff members to complete a risk assessment and, more crucially, to encourage them to use the knowledge gained to take an active role in their health.

Cash, lower employee premium contributions, and employer contributions to the employee's health savings account or flexible spending account are examples of common incentives. Other incentives can be anything from T-shirts or hats to lower deductibles, co-payments, and co-insurance expenses for medical care.

A few businesses compel participation in risk assessments as a condition of receiving health insurance, a practice that carries its own set of legal issues.

7. Programs to Lose Weight: Programs for mental health, physical fitness, and nutrition can all be used to manage obesity in the workplace. There are several options available to employers who are interested in funding weight loss programs for staff members, including the following:

- Providing classes on-site through weight loss companies.

- Granting employees discounts to take lessons away from the workplace.

- Taking part in weight-loss programs offered by colleges, hospitals, and other medical facilities.

- Directing workers to websites run by their insurers that have weight control information.

- Establishing business relationships with suppliers to provide online and telephone-based programs that let staff members interact with coaches to address lifestyle management issues, such as weight control.

- Promoting initiatives like distributing pedometers to workers and asking them to commit to walking 10,000 steps every day

- Exercise routines, fitness facilities, dietary selections, nutritional education, and rewards for joining a weight loss program are all examples of employer-sponsored weight loss initiatives.

8. Programs for Quitting Smoking: Offering programs to help people quit smoking can increase employee longevity and health, reduce healthcare costs, and boost business profits. Such initiatives might consist of the following:

- Requiring a smoke-free environment at work and fostering a quitting culture through powerful marketing and messaging.
- Encouraging tobacco counseling and health risk assessments from the employees' personal physician.
- Pharmaceutical therapy is paid for on a first-dollar basis, which means there are no deductibles or other forms of cost-sharing.
- Eliminating employee co-payments for costs associated with quitting and offering further incentives.

9. Relief From Stress Programs: Employer-sponsored stress reduction programs can help participants recognize when their stress has become unhealthy and has affected aspects of their personal and professional lives, even though stress at a certain level can be a powerful motivator and may boost productivity. Employers should consider stepping up their efforts in wellness programs, given the potentially serious personal and financial costs of excessive stress on employees.

10. Financial Well-being: Financial wellness initiatives frequently target issues like making and adhering to a household budget and taking action to pay long-term debt in an effort to increase employees' "financial literacy." Savings for significant life events like home ownership or paying for college are other topics that are frequently discussed.

11. Health and Wellness Incentives: Employers are increasingly depending on rewards to encourage staff to participate in wellness initiatives and enhance their health-related behaviors.

Employers utilize a variety of incentives to motivate staff to take part in health improvement initiatives. These include making additional donations to health savings accounts as well as providing cash and gift cards. Additionally, some businesses lower their contributions to health plans if workers don't participate in any programs.

According to many experts, reductions in health insurance premiums are the best incentives for motivating employees to participate in wellness programs. Employees may be given such savings, which are increasingly common with companies, in exchange for completing an annual risk assessment, joining a weight loss program, or abstaining from cigarette use.

Employers should ensure that their wellness incentives are created in a way that prevents them from unintentionally encouraging harmful behavior. For instance, a per-pound reward with no upper limit may promote unhealthy methods of weight loss. Alternatively, if an incentive for using a gym expires after a year, staff members can stop going.

Taking Care of a Wellness Program

The success of a wellness program depends on a few key elements. Organizations should take steps to increase employee participation and engagement in wellness programs and activities, in addition to adopting a variety of tested wellness program management strategies.

1. **Increasing Employee Involvement:** Effectively created and managed wellness programs will not succeed without high employee engagement and involvement levels to achieve program objectives.

A more personalized strategy might increase the number of people participating in wellness initiatives. The finest strategies in this regard involve locating prospects and employing deft communication. Organizations can use information from health risk assessments, claims data, or personal health records (including electronic medical records, if accessible) to identify people with an epidemiological need and are open to change. The easiest way to differentiate a participation program is by personalizing messages. HR should work with program providers to create a strategic communications plan that is tailored to the employer's brand, population, and health initiatives.

2. A Rising Level of Employee Engagement: Employee dedication to their wellness, as well as the organization's wellness programs, is referred to as engagement in the context of the wellness program.

Organizations should be aware of the different factors and barriers that can affect engagement in wellness programs, such as the following:

- Family and close friends can be powerful motivators for positive change, but they may also be obstacles because of how much they can affect an employee's behavior.

- Employees require the self-assurance to take the initiative and the tools, materials, and support to do so.

- Senior management, as well as coworkers, can have a significant impact on an employee's decision to participate in worksite initiatives if organizational morale is high.

- Employees demand simple and clear communications about changes to benefits like coverage, cost, and choice.

3. **Communication:** Regardless of the wellness program activities a company chooses to implement, effective communication is essential to achieving the degree of employee engagement and participation required to fulfill the program's objectives. Employers should employ communication to foster a social environment that values good health. This can be accomplished by using tried-and-true marketing strategies that alter behavior, such as the ones listed below:

- An eye-catching program.

- A motto for the wellness program as well as a logo, such as "Everybody Walk Now," "Wellness Wednesday," "Recess," or "Time Out for Tai Chi."

- Visible support and involvement from senior management.

- Employee wellness education based on reliable research.

- Influencing workers based on personal experiences.

4. **Metrics:** Metrics are used to assess the success of wellness programs. Employers should look at both program participation and the return on investment that the company expected when the program was launched.

To really see the return on investment for wellness programs, employers should be ready to wait three to five years. After launching a wellness program, employers should be cautious about making too many adjustments because the more changes made, the more difficult it will be to calculate ROI accurately.

5. Technology: Traditional wellness programs use printed materials, classes given by instructors, and in-person or telephone coaching. All of them can be expensive to deliver and challenging for personnel who work across various locations. The same information may now be provided to an unlimited number of employees, around-the-clock, from any location with an internet connection, and at a fraction of the price using web-based solutions.

Online solutions shouldn't replace offline wellness initiatives; rather, they should be a component of a comprehensive wellness strategy. Online wellness services are offered at a wide range of prices. Online solutions, for instance, can offer support for physical exercise and basic nutrition. Through blogs and bulletin board postings, an open-access website can offer a platform for individuals and groups to establish health goals, monitor their progress, and exchange experiences. Employers can set up private teams and send an email invitation with a link for workers to accept. Online health risk assessments, digital health coaching, illness management and support modules, and automatic, individualized medication, food, and exercise reminders are examples of more advanced options.

Promoting Work-life Balance Awareness

Making sure that your staff members understand the value of work-life balance benefits not just their health but also their productivity and job happiness. Here are some ways small business owners can educate staff members on the need for work-life balance:

1. **Set a Good Example:** As a manager or business owner, set a good example by maintaining a healthy work-life balance. Employees are more likely to cherish their free time when they see their bosses value it.

2. **Define Expectations Clearly:** Specify expectations for working hours, overtime, and communication after business hours. Encourage employees to turn off their work email and phone during personal time.

3. **Flexible Work Arrangements:** When feasible, provide flexible work hours or remote work possibilities. The ability to manage their job in a way that fits their personal lives, such as taking care of family members or engaging in hobbies, is given to employees as a result.

4. Encourage Paid Time Off (PTO): Encourage staff members to utilize their paid time off (PTO), which includes vacation days, holidays, and personal days. Make sure PTO policies are clear and encourage its use for relaxation and rest.

5. Encourage Regular Pauses: Stress the value of taking brief pauses during the workday. To preserve attention and energy, encourage staff members to get up from their workstations during breaks, stretch, and recharge.

6. Promote Mental Health: In order to promote mental health by eradicating the stigma associated with it, encourage staff to seek assistance when necessary by providing resources like Employee Assistance Programs (EAPs).

7. Provide Employee Education: Hold seminars or classes on the advantages of work-life balance. Discuss time management, stress management, and establishing boundaries between your personal and professional lives.

8. Appreciation and Recognition: Show your appreciation for and recognize employees who consistently strike a work-life balance. Highlight their accomplishments and the beneficial effects they have had on their well-being and work output.

9. Promote Hobbies and Interests: Honor employees' interests and hobbies outside the workplace. This can involve planning team-building events centered around their interests or simply recognizing their accomplishments.

10. Wellness Days: Introduce days for wellness or mental health that staff members can use as needed. These times can be spent taking care of oneself, unwinding, or engaging in personal interests.

11. Regular Check-ins: Hold one-on-one meetings with staff members on a regular basis to talk about their workload, stress levels, and general well-being. Use these discussions to provide help and make improvements as required.

12. Establish a Program for Complete Well-being: Address physical, mental, and emotional wellness in your well-being program. To promote a sense of community, incorporate programs like fitness challenges, stress management workshops, mindfulness practices, and social activities.

To sum it up, finding a balance while creating a well-being program for your small business is important. While putting your employees' health and happiness first is imperative, you also need to manage expenditures efficiently. The secret is concentrating on projects that provide the most value for your limited resources. Regularly evaluate these programs' results and make changes in response to employee suggestions and changing wellness trends.

Wellness isn't a luxury in the hectic world of small enterprises; it's an investment in the long-term success of your enterprise.

It's critical to offer advice on what to include and what not to include in a wellness program.

What to Include in Your Well-being Program

1. **Initiatives for Holistic Wellness:** Make sure your program takes into account a variety of well-being factors, such as emotional wellness, social connections, mental wellness, and physical wellness. Think of including these components:

- Fitness programs: Promote physical activity by offering gym memberships, fitness competitions, or group exercise sessions.

- Employee Assistance Programs (EAPs) or counseling services are available to employees who need help with stress, anxiety, or other personal difficulties.

- Stress management: To assist staff in properly managing workplace stress, provide workshops or mindfulness training.

- Nutrition and Healthy Eating: Encourage healthy eating practices by offering wholesome food options at work or hosting informative lectures or cooking workshops.

- **Community Building:** To promote a sense of belonging, plan team-building activities, get-togethers, or volunteer opportunities.

2. Employee Engagement: Actively involve your staff in the wellness initiative. Make participation voluntary, inclusive, and pleasurable while designing projects.

3. Individualization: Take into account the individuality of each worker. Allow for flexible options and individualized wellness programs to suit every person's requirements and preferences.

4. Regular Assessments: Utilize surveys, feedback sessions, and health assessments to continuously review your well-being program's success. Make tweaks and improvements using this information.

5. Leadership Support: Obtain the active and enthusiastic backing of firm executives and managers. Their participation strongly conveys the significance of the program.

6. Communication: Keep lines of communication regarding the goals, advantages, and resources offered by the well-being program transparent and open. Make sure personnel are aware of where to go for assistance or information.

7. Recognition and Rewards: Acknowledge and honor the contributions that employees have made to their well-being. Think about rewarding or praising individuals who contribute actively and accomplish goals.

What Not to Include in Your Well-being Program

1. **Mandatory Participation:** Steer clear of making wellness programs obligatory. Employee resistance and resentment might result from forced engagement.

2. **Invading Programs:** Be considerate of employees' personal space. Avoid using intrusive techniques like monitoring private medical information without permission.

3. **The One-size-fits-all Method:** Recognize that every employee has different needs in terms of well-being. An inflexible, one-size-fits-all strategy that might not accommodate a range of tastes and demands should be avoided.

4. **Excessive Administrative Activities:** Don't overwhelm your HR department or staff with excessive program-related paperwork or administrative activities. Keep procedures simple and accessible.

5. **Excessively Expensive Programs:** While investing in employee well-being is crucial, steer clear of initiatives that go over budget or needlessly tax your resources. Look for affordable solutions.

6. Unrealistic Goals: Establish attainable and sensible objectives for your well-being. A high-pressure environment where employees are under duress to fulfill impossible standards should be avoided.

7. Inadequate Evaluation: Don't forget to evaluate the program's success over time. You won't be able to tell if your efforts are having a favorable effect without an evaluation.

In conclusion, a well-thought-out well-being program can greatly help create a healthier, happier, and more effective workforce. You may build a positive and productive work atmosphere by incorporating holistic activities, involving your staff, and tailoring the program to meet their requirements. In the meantime, it's crucial to stay away from obligatory, intrusive, or excessively expensive strategies that could jeopardize the program's success or employee pleasure. The success of your small business's well-being program depends on finding the appropriate balance between what's best for your employees and for the firm.

www.ingramcontent.com/pod-product-compliance
Lightning Source LLC
Chambersburg PA
CBHW050337010526
44119CB00049B/578